A Touch of Rosie
QUILTS
14 Designs by Carrie L. Nelson

LEISURE ARTS, INC.
Little Rock, Arkansas

EDITORIAL STAFF

EDITOR-IN-CHIEF: Susan White Sullivan
CRAFT PUBLICATIONS DIRECTOR: Cheryl Johnson
SPECIAL PROJECTS DIRECTOR: Susan Frantz Wiles
SENIOR PREPRESS DIRECTOR: Mark Hawkins
ART PUBLICATIONS DIRECTOR: Rhonda Shelby
TECHNICAL EDITOR: Lisa Lancaster
TECHNICAL WRITER: Frances Huddleston
TECHNICAL ASSOCIATE: Mary Hutcheson
EDITORIAL WRITER: Susan McManus Johnson
ART CATEGORY MANAGER: Lora Puls
GRAPHIC DESIGNER: Amy Temple
GRAPHIC ARTISTS: Becca Snider, Angela Ormsby Stark,
    and Janie Marie Wright
IMAGING TECHNICIANS: Stephanie Johnson
    and Mark R. Potter
PHOTOGRAPHY MANAGER: Katherine Laughlin
CONTRIBUTING PHOTOGRAPHER: Ken West
PUBLISHING SYSTEMS ADMINISTRATOR: Becky Riddle
MAC INFORMATION TECHNOLOGY SPECIALIST:
    Robert Young

BUSINESS STAFF

PRESIDENT AND CHIEF EXECUTIVE OFFICER: Rick Barton
VICE PRESIDENT AND CHIEF OPERATIONS OFFICER:
    Tom Siebenmorgen
DIRECTOR OF FINANCE AND ADMINISTRATION:
    Laticia Mull Dittrich
NATIONAL SALES DIRECTOR: Martha Adams
INFORMATION TECHNOLOGY DIRECTOR: Hermine Linz
CONTROLLER: Francis Caple
VICE PRESIDENT, OPERATIONS: Jim Dittrich
RETAIL CUSTOMER SERVICE MANAGER: Stan Raynor
PRINT PRODUCTION MANAGER: Fred F. Pruss

Library of Congress Control Number: 2010927400
ISBN-13: 978-1-60900-013-4

Table of CONTENTS

Designer
CARRIE NELSON

Quilts that capture your heart and imagination—you know right away they're quilts by Carrie L. Nelson. And when you realize that Carrie's favorite inspiration for these playful creations is a lovable golden retriever named Rosie, you understand how every quilt in this collection is just that—a little bit "rosie." To further carry out the theme, there is a touch of pink or red fabric in each of these amazing fabric compositions. You'll also find Carrie's amusing notes on how she was inspired to develop and name each quilt. It's a fun way to visit with Carrie as you choose your favorite fabrics and make your own versions of these darling designs!

Full BLOOM

Quilted by Diane Tricka.

Finished Quilt Size:
80" x 80" (203 cm x 203 cm)
Finished Block Size:
13^1/$_2$" x 13^1/$_2$" (34 cm x 34 cm)

It seems as though some quilts start with a definite plan—that may or may not be followed completely—while others just kind of happen. Then there are the quilts that have a mind of their own. No matter what kind of plan I may have to start with, the finished quilt is the result of enough changes that I almost forget what it was I started out trying to do.

Here was the original plan: I wanted the red and lilac to be somewhat planned. I wanted the pastels and background prints to be even less planned. The thing is, the red had other plans. Fortunately, I had the perfect antidote—a seam ripper! Let it suffice to say that I have a couple of leftover nine patches that I hadn't anticipated.

The name of this quilt was inspired by a wonderful quote from the writings of Anaïs Nin, "…and then the day came when the risk to remain tight inside a bud became more painful than the risk it took to blossom."

YARDAGE REQUIREMENTS

Yardage is based on 43"/44" (109 cm/112 cm) wide fabric. Fat quarters are approximately 21" x 18" (53 cm x 46 cm).

- 10 fat quarters of assorted light print fabrics
- 16 fat quarters of assorted medium print fabrics (pinks, yellows, and greens)
- 4 fat quarters of assorted red print fabrics
- 4 fat quarters of assorted lilac print fabrics
- $^7/_8$ yd (80 cm) of fabric for binding
- $7^3/_8$ yds (6.7 m) of fabric for backing

You will also need:

- 88" x 88" (224 cm x 224 cm) piece of batting
- EZ Quilting® Tri-Recs™ Tools *or* template plastic

CUTTING OUT THE PIECES

*Follow **Rotary Cutting**, page 105, to cut fabric. All measurements include $^1/_4$" seam allowances. Use Tri-Recs™ Tools or make templates from triangle patterns, page 10, to cut background triangles and star point triangles.*

From *each* of 9 assorted light print fat quarters:

- Cut 1 strip 5" x 21". From this strip,
  - Using the Tri Tool or template, cut 6 **background triangles**. Cut a total of 48 background triangles.
- Cut 1 strip $5^3/_8$" x 21". From this strip,
  - Cut 3 **large squares** $5^3/_8$" x $5^3/_8$". Cut a total of 24 large squares.
- Cut 3 **strips** 2" x 21". Cut a total of 27 strips.

From remaining light print fat quarter:

- Cut 8 **strips** 2" x 21". You will have 35 light print strips.
  - Choose 15 of these 35 strips for inner borders. From *each* of these 15 strips,
    - Cut 2 **border strips** 2" x $10^1/_2$". You will have 30 border strips.

From *each* assorted medium print fat quarter:

- Cut 1 strip $5^3/_8$" x 21". From this strip,
  - Cut 2 **large squares** $5^3/_8$" x $5^3/_8$". Cut a total of 24 large squares.
  - Cut 1 **small square** 5" x 5". Cut a total of 16 small squares.
- Cut 2 strips 5" x 21". From these strips,
  - Cut 8 **small squares** 5" x 5". Cut a total of 117 small squares. You will have 133 small squares.
- Cut 1 strip 2" x 21". From this strip,
  - Cut 3 **rectangles** 2" x 5". Cut a total of 44 rectangles.

From *each* assorted red print fat quarter:

- Cut 7 **strips** 2" x 21". Cut a total of 25 strips.

From *each* assorted lilac print fat quarter:

- Cut 3 strips 5" x 21". From *each* strip,
  - Using the Recs Tool or template, cut 4 **star point triangles** and 4 **star point triangles in reverse**. Cut a total of 48 star point triangles and 48 star point triangles in reverse.

MAKING THE STAR POINT UNITS

*Follow **Piecing**, page 106, and **Pressing**, page 107, to assemble quilt top. Because there are so many seams in this quilt, you may need to use a seam allowance slightly smaller than the usual $^1/_4$". As you sew, measure your work to compare with the measurements provided, which include seam allowances, and adjust your seam allowance as needed. Arrows on diagrams indicate suggested directions to press seam allowances.*

1. For each **Star Point Unit**, select 1 **star point triangle** and 1 **star point triangle in reverse** from 1 fabric and 1 **background triangle**.
2. Referring to **Fig. 1**, sew **star point triangle** to left side of **background triangle**; sew **star point triangle in reverse** to right side to make **Star Point Unit**. Each Star Point Unit should measure 5" x 5".

Fig. 1

3. Repeat **Steps 1–2** to make 48 Star Point Units.

Star Point Unit (make 48)

MAKING THE TRIANGLE-SQUARES

1. Draw a diagonal line (corner to corner) on wrong side of each light **large square**.
2. Matching right sides, place 1 light **large square** on top of 1 medium print **large square**. Stitch ¹/₄" from each side of drawn line (**Fig. 2**). Cut along drawn line and press seam allowances to medium print to make 2 **Triangle-Squares**. Each Triangle-Square should measure 5" x 5". Make 48 Triangle-Squares.

Fig. 2

Triangle-Square (make 48)

MAKING THE NINE PATCHES

1. Sew 2 red **strips** and 1 light **strip** together to make **Strip Set A**. Strip Set A should measure 21" x 5". Make 10 Strip Set A's. Cut across Strip Set A's at 2" intervals to make 96 **Unit 1's**. Unit 1 should measure 2" x 5".

Strip Set A   **Unit 1**
(make 10)   (make 96)

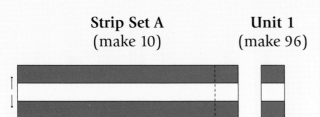

2. Sew 2 light **strips** and 1 red **strip** together to make **Strip Set B**. Strip Set B should measure 21" x 5". Make 5 Strip Set B's. Cut across Strip Set B's at 2" intervals to make 48 **Unit 2's**. Unit 2 should measure 2" x 5".

Strip Set B   **Unit 2**
(make 5)   (make 48)

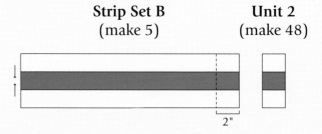

3. Sew 2 **Unit 1's** and 1 **Unit 2** together to make **Nine Patch**. Nine Patch should measure 5" x 5". Make 48 Nine Patches.

Nine Patch (make 48)

MAKING THE STAR BLOCKS

1. Sew 2 **Triangle Squares** and 1 **Star Point Unit** together to make **Unit 3**. Make 24 Unit 3's.

Unit 3 (make 24)

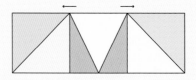

2. Sew 2 **Star Point Units** and 1 **Nine Patch** together to make **Unit 4**. Make 12 Unit 4's.

Unit 4 (make 12)

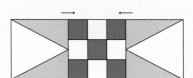

3. Sew 2 **Unit 3's** and 1 **Unit** 4 together to make **Star Block**. Block should measure 14" x 14". Make 12 Star Blocks.

Star Block (make 12)

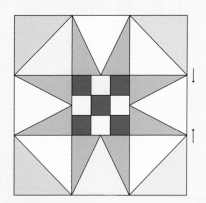

MAKING THE COMPOUND NINE PATCH BLOCKS

1. Sew 1 **Nine Patch** and 2 **small squares** together to make **Unit 5**. Make 16 Unit 5's.

Unit 5 (make 16)

2. Sew 1 **Nine Patch** and 2 **small squares** together to make **Unit 6**. Make 8 Unit 6's.

Unit 6 (make 8)

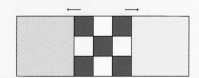

3. Sew 2 **Unit 5's** and 1 **Unit 6** together to make **Compound Nine Patch Block A**. Block should measure 14" x 14". Make 8 Compound Nine Patch Block A's.

Compound Nine Patch Block A (make 8)

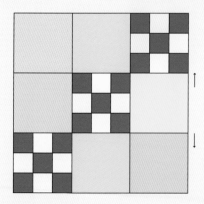

4. Sew 3 **small squares** together to make **Unit 7**. Make 4 Unit 7's.

Unit 7 (make 4)

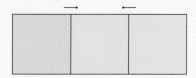

5. Sew 1 **Nine Patch** and 2 **small squares** together to make **Unit 8**. Make 4 Unit 8's.

Unit 8 (make 4)

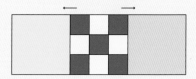

6. Sew 2 **Nine Patches** and 1 **small square** together to make **Unit 9**. Make 4 Unit 9's.

Unit 9 (make 4)

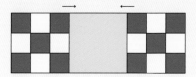

7. Sew 1 **Unit 7**, 1 **Unit 8**, and 1 **Unit 9** together to make **Compound Nine Patch Block B**. Block should measure 14" x 14". Make 4 Compound Nine Patch Block B's.

Compound Nine Patch Block B (make 4)

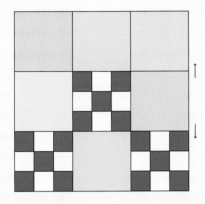

MAKING THE NINE PATCH BLOCK

1. Sew 3 **small squares** together to make **Unit 10**. Make 3 Unit 10's.

Unit 10 (make 3)

2. Sew 3 **Unit 10's** together to make **Nine Patch Block**. Block should measure 14" x 14".

Nine Patch Block

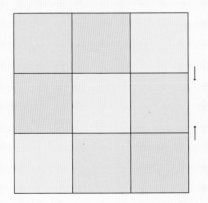

ASSEMBLING THE QUILT TOP CENTER

Refer to Quilt Top Diagram, page 11, for placement.

1. Sew 3 **Star Blocks** and 2 **Compound Nine Patch Block A's** together to make **Row A**. Press seam allowances open or to Compound Nine Patch Blocks. Row A should measure 68" x 14". Make 2 Row A's.

2. Sew 2 **Compound Nine Patch Block A's**, 2 **Star Blocks**, and 1 **Compound Nine Patch Block B** together to make **Row B**. Press seam allowances open or to Compound Nine Patch Blocks. Row B should measure 68" x 14". Make 2 Row B's.

3. Sew 2 **Star Blocks**, 2 **Compound Nine Patch Block B's** and 1 **Nine Patch Block** together to make **Row C**. Press seam allowances open or to Compound Nine Patch Blocks. Row C should measure 68" x 14".

4. Sew **Rows** together, pressing seam allowances open or in one direction. Quilt top center should measure 68" x 68".

ADDING THE INNER BORDER

1. Sew 7 **border strips** together to make **side inner border**. Press seam allowances open or in one direction. Make 2 side inner borders.

2. Measure *length* across center of quilt top center. Trim inner side borders to determined length. Matching centers and corners, sew side inner borders to quilt top center.

3. Sew 8 **border strips** together to make **top inner border**. Press seam allowances open or in one direction. Repeat to make **bottom inner border**.

4. Measure *width* across center of quilt top center (including added borders). Trim top/bottom inner borders to determined length. Matching centers and corners, sew top/bottom inner borders to quilt top center. Press seam allowances to inner borders.

Adding the Outer Border

1. Sew 12 **small squares** and 11 **rectangles** together to make **outer border**. Press seam allowances to squares. Make 4 outer borders.

2. Measure *length* across center of quilt top. Measure length of 2 outer borders. If measurements are not the same, make seams in borders slightly larger or smaller as needed for **side outer borders**. Do not sew side outer borders to quilt top at this time.

3. Measure *width* across center of quilt top. Measure length of 2 remaining outer borders. If measurements are not the same, make seams in borders slightly larger or smaller as needed for **top/bottom outer borders**. Sew 1 **small square** to each end of top/bottom borders. Do not sew top/bottom borders to quilt top at this time.

4. Matching centers and corners, sew side and then top and bottom outer borders to quilt top. Press seam allowances to outer border. Quilt top should measure 80" x 80".

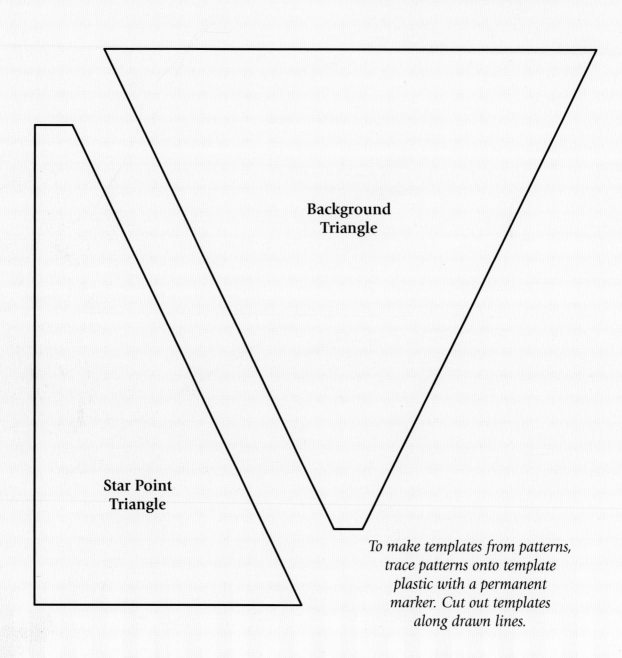

Background Triangle

Star Point Triangle

To make templates from patterns, trace patterns onto template plastic with a permanent marker. Cut out templates along drawn lines.

COMPLETING THE QUILT

. To help stabilize the edges and prevent any seams from separating, stay-stitch around the quilt top approximately $1/8$" from the edge.

. Follow **Machine Quilting**, page 107, to mark, layer, and quilt as desired. Quilt shown was machine quilted. The Blocks and inner border were quilted in the ditch. A curved line pattern was quilted with red thread in the small Nine Patches. Fanning lines were quilted in the light portions of the Triangle-Squares and in the Star Point Units, with lilac thread used in the lilac areas. A feather pattern was quilted in the medium print areas of the Blocks. A "Z" pattern was quilted in the inner border and a swirling pattern was quilted in the outer border.

3. Follow **Making a Hanging Sleeve**, page 109, if a hanging sleeve is desired.

4. Cut a 28" square of binding fabric. Follow **Binding**, page 109, to bind quilt using 2"w bias binding with mitered corners.

NOTE: This quilt can be made larger or smaller, but it will require adding or subtracting 2 vertical Rows or horizontal Rows. This will change the measurement of the quilt by 27". To make the quilt slightly larger, add a pieced or plain border.

Quilt Top Diagram

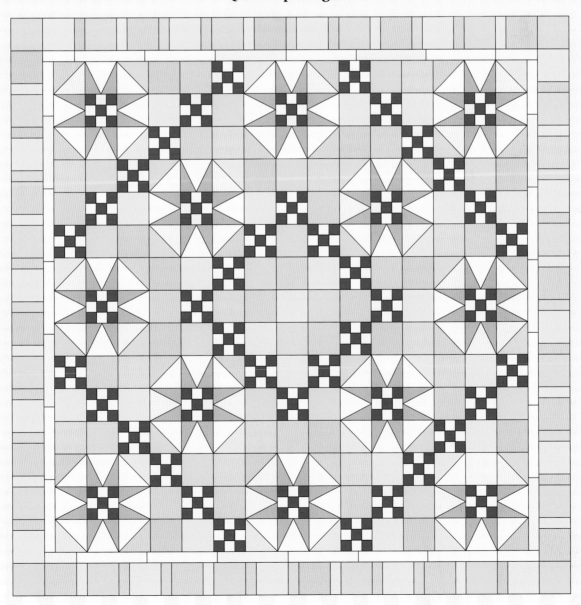

High COTTON

Pieced by Mary Dyer.
Quilted by Linda DeVries.

Finished Quilt Size:
72¹/₂" x 84¹/₂" (184 cm x 215 cm)
Finished Block Size:
12" x 12" (30 cm x 30 cm)

Whatever style of fabric you use, the goal here is to capture the feeling of summertime. The air is sweet whether you're enjoying a hot, sunny day spent under the shade of a big tree, or a soft warm evening under a blanket of stars.

I loved this fabric, but didn't have a clue what to make. Of course, I bought it anyway. I had some leftover triangle-squares from class demo pieces and started thinking of blocks that might work, when—Shazaam!—I got an idea! Each block has sashing pieces sewn to just two sides.

Since I was thinking about summertime, the song by that name from the play Porgy and Bess came to mind. The lyrics helped me name the quilt. "Summertime, and the livin' is easy. Fish are jumpin' and the cotton is high…."

Soft and sweet. It's just the kind of quilt I wanted.

YARDAGE REQUIREMENTS

Yardage is based on 43"/44" (109 cm/112 cm) wide fabric. Fat quarters are approximately 21" x 18" (53 cm x 46 cm).

- 11 fat quarters of assorted light print fabrics for backgrounds
- 24 fat quarters of assorted "dark" print fabrics (darker than the light print fabrics)
- $7/8$ yd (80 cm) of fabric for binding
- $6^3/4$ yds (6.2 m)* of fabric for backing

You will also need:

- 81" x 93" (206 cm x 236 cm) piece of batting

*Yardage is based on three 81" (206 cm) lengths of fabric, which allows for a larger backing for long arm quilting. If you are using another quilting method, two 93" (236 cm) lengths or $5^1/4$ yds (4.8 m), will be adequate.

CUTTING OUT THE PIECES

*Follow **Rotary Cutting**, page 105, to cut fabric. All measurements include $1/4$" seam allowances.*

From *each* assorted light print fat quarter:

- Cut 1 strip $3^7/8$" x 21". From this strip,
  - Cut 5 **large squares** $3^7/8$" x $3^7/8$". Cut a total of 55 large squares.
- Cut 1 strip $3^7/8$" x 21". From this strip,
  - Cut 1 **large square** $3^7/8$" x $3^7/8$". Cut a total of 5 large squares. You will have 60 (30 sets of 2 matching) large squares.

  From remainder of strip,
  - Cut 1 strip $3^1/2$" x $17^1/8$". From this strip,
    - Cut 4 **medium squares** $3^1/2$" x $3^1/2$". Cut a total of 44 medium squares.
- Cut 1 strip $3^1/2$" x 21". From this strip,
  - Cut 5 **medium squares** $3^1/2$" x $3^1/2$". Cut a total of 52 medium squares. You will have 96 (22 sets of 4 matching and 8 assorted) medium squares.
- Cut 1 **strip** 2" x 21". Cut a total of 9 strips.
- Cut 1 strip $1^7/8$" x 21". From this strip,
  - Cut 2 sets, each with these matching pieces: 2 **small squares** $1^7/8$" x $1^7/8$" and 4 **very small squares** $1^1/2$" x $1^1/2$". Cut a total of 15 sets.

From *each* assorted dark print fat quarter:

- Cut 1 strip $6^7/8$" x 21". From this strip,
  - Cut 2 **very large squares** $6^7/8$" x $6^7/8$". Cut a total of 48 very large squares.

  From remainder of strip,
  - Cut 2 **medium squares** $3^1/2$" x $3^1/2$". Cut a total of 48 medium squares.
- Cut 1 strip $3^7/8$" x 21". From this strip,
  - Cut 5 **large squares** $3^7/8$" x $3^7/8$". Cut a total of 120 large squares.
- Cut 1 strip $3^7/8$" x 21". From this strip,
  - Cut 4 **large squares** $3^7/8$" x $3^7/8$". Cut a total of 80 large squares. You will have 200 (30 sets of 2 matching plus 140 assorted) large squares.
  - Cut 1 **medium square** $3^1/2$" x $3^1/2$". Cut a total of 19 medium squares. You will have a total of 67 medium squares.
- From *each* of 9 prints,
  - Cut 1 **strip** 2" x 21". Cut a total of 9 strips.
- From *each* of remaining 15 prints,
  - Cut 1 set with these matching pieces: 2 **small squares** $1^7/8$" x $1^7/8$" and 1 **very small square** $1^1/2$" x $1^1/2$". Cut a total of 15 sets.

MAKING THE SHOOFLY A'S

*Follow **Piecing**, page 106, and **Pressing**, page 107, to assemble quilt top. Because there are so many seams in this quilt, you may need to use a seam allowance slightly smaller than the usual $1/4$". As you sew, measure your work to compare with the measurements provided, which include seam allowances, and adjust your seam allowance as needed. Arrows on diagrams indicate suggested directions to press seam allowances.*

1. For **Shoofly A**, select 2 **large squares**, 1 **medium square**, and 1 **strip** from 1 light print; select 2 **large squares** and 1 **strip** from 1 dark print.
2. Draw a diagonal line (corner to corner) on wrong side of each light **large square**.

. Matching right sides, place 1 light **large square** on top of 1 dark **large square**. Stitch $^1/_4$" from each side of drawn line (**Fig. 1**). Cut along drawn line and press seam allowances to dark fabric to make 2 **Medium Triangle-Squares**. Medium Triangle-Square should measure $3^1/_2$" x $3^1/_2$". Make 4 Medium Triangle-Squares.

Fig. 1

Medium Triangle-Square (make 4)

. Sew 1 light **strip** and 1 dark **strip** together to make **Strip Set**. Press seam allowances to dark strip. Strip Set should measure 21" x $3^1/_2$". Cut across **Strip Set** at $3^1/_2$" intervals to make 4 **Unit 1's**. Unit 1 should measure $3^1/_2$" x $3^1/_2$". *Set remainder of Strip Set aside for later use.*

Strip Set

Unit 1 (make 4)

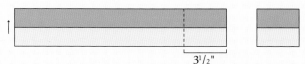

$3^1/_2$"

Sew 2 **Medium Triangle-Squares** and 1 **Unit 1** together to make **Unit 2**. Make 2 Unit 2's.

Unit 2 (make 2)

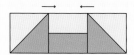

6. Sew 2 **Unit 1's** and light **medium square** together to make **Unit 3**.

Unit 3

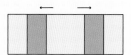

7. Sew 2 **Unit 2's** and **Unit 3** together to make **Shoofly A**. Shoofly A should measure $9^1/_2$" x $9^1/_2$".

8 Repeat **Steps 1–7** to make 8 Shoofly A's.

Shoofly A (make 8)

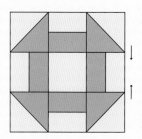

MAKING THE SHOOFLY B'S

1. For **Shoofly B**, select 2 **large squares** and 4 **medium squares** from 1 light print; select 2 **large squares** and 1 **medium square** from 1 dark print.

2. In the same manner as before and using the **large squares**, make 4 **Medium Triangle-Squares**. Medium Triangle-Square should measure $3^1/_2$" x $3^1/_2$".

Medium Triangle-Square (make 4)

3. Sew 2 **Medium Triangle-Squares** and 1 light **medium square** together to make **Unit 4**. Make 2 Unit 4's.

Unit 4 (make 2)

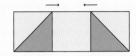

4. Sew 2 light **medium squares** and 1 dark **medium square** together to make **Unit 5**.

Unit 5

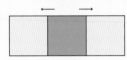

5. Sew 2 **Unit 4's** and **Unit 5** together to make **Shoofly B**. Shoofly B should measure $9^1/_2$" x $9^1/_2$".

6. Repeat **Steps 1–5** to make 22 Shoofly B's.

Shoofly B (make 22)

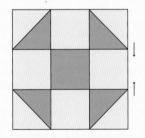

MAKING THE BLOCK SASHINGS

1. Draw a diagonal line (corner to corner) on wrong side of 70 dark **large squares**.

2. Matching right sides, place 1 marked dark **large square** on top of 1 unmarked dark **large square**. In the same manner as before, make 140 **Medium Triangle-Squares**. Medium Triangle-Square should measure $3^1/_2$" x $3^1/_2$".

Medium Triangle-Square (make 140)

3. For **Small Shoofly**, select 1 set of 2 **small squares** and 4 **very small squares** from 1 light print; select 1 set of 2 **small squares** and 1 **very small square** from 1 dark print.

4. Draw a diagonal line (corner to corner) on wrong side of each light **small square**.

5. In the same manner as before and using **small squares**, make 4 **Small Triangle-Squares**. Small Triangle-Square should measure $1^1/_2$" x $1^1/_2$".

Small Triangle-Square (make 4)

6. Sew 2 **Small Triangle-Squares** and 1 light **very small square** together to make **Unit 6**. Make 2 Unit 6's.

Unit 6 (make 2)

7. Sew 2 light **very small squares** and 1 dark **very small square** together to make **Unit 7**.

Unit 7

8. Sew 2 **Unit 6's** and **Unit 7** together to make **Small Shoofly**. Small Shoofly should measure $3^1/_2$" x $3^1/_2$".

9. Repeat **Steps 3–8** to make 15 Small Shooflies.

Small Shoofly (make 15)

10. Sew remaining **light strip** and **dark strip** together to make **Strip Set**. Press seam allowances to dark strip. Strip Set should measure 21" x 3¹/₂".

Strip Set

11. For **Four Patch**, select this **Strip Set** *or* remainder of one of the **Strip Sets** put aside earlier. Cut across Strip Set at 2" intervals to make 2 **Unit 8's**. Unit 8 should measure 2" x 3¹/₂".

Unit 8 (make 2)

12. Sew 2 **Unit 8's** together to make **Four Patch**. To press seam allowances, follow **Collapsing the Seams**, page 107. Four Patch should measure 3¹/₂" x 3¹/₂".

13. Repeat **Steps 11–12** to make 10 Four Patches.

Four Patch (make 10)

14. Select 3 in any combination of **Medium Triangle-Squares**, **Small Shooflies**, **Four Patches**, and dark **medium squares**. Sew pieces together to make **short sashing**. Short sashing should measure 3¹/₂" x 9¹/₂". Make 30 short sashings.

Short Sashing (make 30)

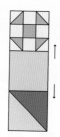

15. Select 4 in any combination of **Medium Triangle-Squares**, **Small Shooflies**, **Four Patches**, and dark **medium squares**. Sew pieces together to make **long sashing**. Long sashing should measure 3¹/₂" x 12¹/₂". Make 30 long sashings.

Long Sashing (make 30)

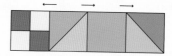

Making the Blocks

1. For **Block**, select 1 **Shoofly A** *or* **Shoofly B**, 1 **long sashing**, and 1 **short sashing**.

2. Sew **Shoofly** and 1 **short sashing** together to make **Unit 9**.

Unit 9

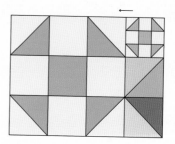

3. Sew **Unit 9** and **long sashing** together to make **Block**. Block should measure 12¹/₂" x 12¹/₂".

4. Repeat **Steps 1–3** to make 30 Blocks.

Block (make 30)

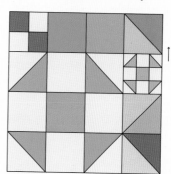

ASSEMBLING THE QUILT TOP CENTER

*Refer to **Assembly Diagram** to assemble quilt top center.*

1. Rotating every other Block, sew 5 **Blocks** together to make **Row**. Press seam allowances open or press them in one direction in every other Row and in the opposite direction in remaining Rows. Row should measure $60^1/2$" x $12^1/2$". Make 6 Rows.
2. Sew **Rows** together, pressing seam allowances open or in one direction. Quilt top center should measure $60^1/2$" x $72^1/2$".

ADDING THE BORDER

1. Draw a diagonal line (corner to corner) on wrong side of 24 dark **very large squares**.
2. Matching right sides, place 1 marked dark **very large square** on top of 1 unmarked dark **very large square**. In the same manner as before, make 48 **Large Triangle-Squares**. Large Triangle-Square should measure $6^1/2$" x $6^1/2$".

Large Triangle-Square (make 48)

3. Sew 12 **Large Triangle-Squares** together to make **border**. Press seam allowances open or in one direction. Make 4 borders.
4. Measure *length* across center of quilt top center. Measure length of 2 borders. If measurements are not the same, make seams in borders slightly larger or smaller as needed for **side borders**. Matching centers and corners, sew side borders to quilt top. Press seam allowances open or to borders.
5. Measure *width* across center of quilt top center (including added borders). Measure length of 2 remaining borders. If measurements are not the same, make seams in borders slightly larger or smaller as needed for **top/bottom borders**. Matching centers and corners, sew top/bottom border to quilt top. Press seam allowances open or to borders. Quilt top should measure $72^1/2$" x $84^1/2$".

COMPLETING THE QUILT

1. To help stabilize the edges and prevent any seams from separating, stay-stitch around the quilt top approximately $1/8$" from the edge.
2. Follow **Machine Quilting**, page 107, to mark, layer, and quilt as desired. Quilt shown was machine quilted with a looping pattern in the large Shooflies. The sashings were quilted with a curved triangle in each half of the Triangle-Squares, a curved square in each Small Shoofly and in each square of the Four Patches, and a feather pattern in each medium square. The border was quilted with a feather in each half of each Triangle-Square.
3. Follow **Making a Hanging Sleeve**, page 109, if a hanging sleeve is desired.
4. Cut a 28" square of binding fabric. Follow **Binding**, page 109, to bind quilt using 2"w bias binding with mitered corners.

NOTE: This quilt can be made larger or smaller by adding or subtracting vertical Rows or horizontal Rows. Each Row will change the measurement of the quilt by 12".

Summer WIND

Quilted by Louise Haley.
Binding applied by Sue Maitre.

Finished Quilt Size:
76$\frac{1}{2}$" x 76$\frac{1}{2}$" (194 cm x 194 cm)

Summer is my favorite time of year, even living here in Arizona. I love the heat, especially when it gets hot enough that you feel "warm in your bones." Accordingly, I love anything that looks and feels like summer—especially quilts.

Considering how many quilts I make that have pieced borders, I think this one was inevitable. After all, it is just one big star and then row after row of pieced borders.

Whether you make this design using soft, pastel floral prints or something more vibrant, this quilt will work with any color scheme and fabric style. Just pick an accent color, a few background prints, and a whole bunch of fabrics in complementary color groups and you're all set to go—in any season.

Yardage Requirements

Yardage is based on 43"/44" (109 cm/112 cm) wide fabric. Fat quarters are approximately 21" x 18" (53 cm x 46 cm).

   9 fat quarters of assorted cream print fabrics
   4 fat quarters of assorted blue print fabrics
   $^3/_8$ yd (34 cm) *or* 2 matching fat quarters of pink print fabric
   19 fat quarters of assorted pastel (pink, yellow, and green) print fabrics
   $^7/_8$ yd (80 cm) of fabric for binding
   $7^1/_8$ yds (6.5 m) of fabric for backing

You will also need:
   85" x 85" (216 cm x 216 cm) piece of batting

Cutting Out the Pieces

*Follow **Rotary Cutting**, page 105, to cut fabric. All measurements include $^1/_4$" seam allowances.*

From 1 cream print fat quarter:
- Cut 1 **square C** $11^1/_4$" x $11^1/_4$".

From a 2nd cream print fat quarter:
- Cut 1 strip $11^1/_4$" x 21". From this strip,
  - Cut 1 **square C** $11^1/_4$" x $11^1/_4$".
  - Cut 4 **squares I** $2^1/_2$" x $2^1/_2$".
- Cut 2 strips $2^7/_8$" x 21". From these strips,
  - Cut 12 **squares G** $2^7/_8$" x $2^7/_8$".

From a 3rd cream print fat quarter:
- Cut 1 strip $6^7/_8$" x 21". From this strip,
  - Cut 2 **squares E** $6^7/_8$" x $6^7/_8$".
- Cut 1 strip $5^1/_4$" x 21". From this strip,
  - Cut 4 **squares P** $5^1/_4$" x $5^1/_4$".
- Cut 2 strips $2^1/_2$" x 21". From these strips,
  - Cut 16 **squares I** $2^1/_2$" x $2^1/_2$".

From *each* of 2 assorted cream print fat quarters:
- Cut 1 strip $5^1/_4$" x 21". From this strip,
  - Cut 4 **squares P** $5^1/_4$" x $5^1/_4$". Cut a total of 8 squares P.
- Cut 1 strip $4^1/_4$" x 21". From this strip,
  - Cut 3 **squares L** $4^1/_4$" x $4^1/_4$". Cut a total of 6 squares L.
  - Cut 1 **square M** $3^7/_8$" x $3^7/_8$". Cut a total of 2 squares M.
- Cut 2 strips $2^1/_2$" x 21". From these strips,
  - Cut 16 **squares I** $2^1/_2$" x $2^1/_2$". Cut a total of 32 squares I.

From *each* of 4 assorted cream print fat quarters:
- Cut 1 strip $5^1/_4$" x 21". From this strip,
  - Cut 3 **squares P** $5^1/_4$" x $5^1/_4$". Cut a total of 12 squares P. You will have 24 squares P.
- Cut 1 strip $4^1/_4$" x 21". From this strip,
  - Cut 4 **squares L** $4^1/_4$" x $4^1/_4$". Cut a total of 14 squares L. You will have 20 squares L.
- Cut 1 strip $2^7/_8$" x 21". From this strip,
  - Cut 6 **squares G** $2^7/_8$" x $2^7/_8$". Cut a total of 24 squares G. You will have 36 (1 set of 12 matching, 4 sets of 4 matching, and 4 sets of 2 matching) squares G.
- Cut 2 strips $2^1/_2$" x 21". From these strips,
  - Cut 16 **squares I** $2^1/_2$" x $2^1/_2$". Cut a total of 64 squares I. You will have 116 (29 sets of 4 matching) squares I.

From *each* assorted blue print fat quarter:
- Cut 1 strip $5^1/_4$" x 21". From this strip,
  - Cut 1 **square S** $5^1/_4$" x $5^1/_4$". Cut a total of 4 squares S.
  - Cut 1 **square T** $4^1/_2$" x $4^1/_2$". Cut a total of 4 squares T.
  - Cut 1 **square K** $4^1/_4$" x $4^1/_4$". Cut a total of 4 squares K.
  - Cut 1 **square N** $3^7/_8$" x $3^7/_8$". Cut a total of 2 squares N.
- Cut 1 strip $4^1/_4$" x 21". From this strip,
  - Cut 4 **squares K** $4^1/_4$" x $4^1/_4$". Cut a total of 16 squares K. You will have 20 squares K.
- Cut 1 strip $2^7/_8$" x 21". From this strip,
  - Cut 6 **squares H** $2^7/_8$" x $2^7/_8$". Cut a total of 20 (3 sets of 4 matching and 4 sets of 2 matching) squares H.

From pink print yardage or 2 matching fat quarters:

- Cut 2 **squares D** $11^{1}/_{4}$" x $11^{1}/_{4}$".

From 1 pastel (pink) print fat quarter:

- Cut 1 strip $7^{1}/_{2}$" x 21". From this strip,
  - Cut 1 **square A** $7^{1}/_{2}$" x $7^{1}/_{2}$".
  - Cut 1 **square W** $6^{1}/_{2}$" x $6^{1}/_{2}$".
- Cut 1 strip $4^{7}/_{8}$" x 21". From this strip,
  - Cut 4 **squares O** $4^{7}/_{8}$" x $4^{7}/_{8}$".

From a 2nd pastel (green) print fat quarter:

- Cut 1 strip $6^{1}/_{4}$" x 21". From this strip,
  - Cut 2 squares $6^{1}/_{4}$" x $6^{1}/_{4}$". Cut squares *once* diagonally to make 4 **triangles B**. (These are slightly larger than needed and will be trimmed.)
- Cut 1 strip $6^{1}/_{2}$" x 21". From this strip,
  - Cut 2 **squares W** $6^{1}/_{2}$" x $6^{1}/_{2}$".

From a 3rd pastel (yellow) print fat quarter:

- Cut 1 strip $6^{7}/_{8}$" x 21". From this strip,
  - Cut 2 **squares F** $6^{7}/_{8}$" x $6^{7}/_{8}$".
- Cut 1 **square W** $6^{1}/_{2}$" x $6^{1}/_{2}$". You will have 4 squares W.

From *each* of 12 assorted pastel print fat quarters:

- Cut 1 strip $6^{1}/_{2}$" x 21". From this strip,
  - Cut 1 **rectangle U** $6^{1}/_{2}$" x $8^{1}/_{2}$". Cut a total of 12 rectangles U.
  - Cut 2 **rectangles V** $6^{1}/_{2}$" x $4^{1}/_{2}$". Cut a total of 24 rectangles V.
- Cut 1 strip $2^{7}/_{8}$" x 21". From this strip,
  - Cut 7 **squares Q** $2^{7}/_{8}$" x $2^{7}/_{8}$". Cut a total of 84 squares Q.
- Cut 1 strip $2^{7}/_{8}$" x 21". From this strip,
  - Cut 1 **square Q** $2^{7}/_{8}$" x $2^{7}/_{8}$". Cut a total of 12 squares Q. You will have 96 (24 sets of 4 matching) squares Q.
  - Cut 7 **squares J** $2^{1}/_{2}$" x $2^{1}/_{2}$". Cut a total of 84 squares J.
- Cut 1 strip $4^{7}/_{8}$" x 21". From this strip,
  - Cut 2 **squares O** $4^{7}/_{8}$" x $4^{7}/_{8}$". Cut a total of 24 squares O.
  - Cut 2 **squares R** $4^{1}/_{2}$" x $4^{1}/_{2}$". Cut a total of 24 squares R.

From *each* of 4 assorted pastel print fat quarters:

- Cut 1 strip $6^{1}/_{2}$" x 21". From this strip,
  - Cut 1 **rectangle U** $6^{1}/_{2}$" x $8^{1}/_{2}$". Cut a total of 4 rectangles U. You will have 16 rectangles U.
  - Cut 2 **rectangles V** $6^{1}/_{2}$" x $4^{1}/_{2}$". Cut a total of 8 rectangles V. You will have 32 rectangles V.
- Cut 1 strip $4^{7}/_{8}$" x 21". From this strip,
  - Cut 4 **squares O** $4^{7}/_{8}$" x $4^{7}/_{8}$". Cut a total of 16 squares O. You will have 44 squares O.
- Cut 2 strips $2^{1}/_{2}$" x 21". From these strips,
  - Cut 12 **squares J** $2^{1}/_{2}$" x $2^{1}/_{2}$". Cut a total of 48 squares J. You will have 132 squares J.

MAKING THE STAR CENTER

Follow Piecing, page 106, and Pressing, page 107, to assemble the quilt top. Because there are so many seams in this quilt, you may need to use a seam allowance slightly smaller than the usual $^{1}/_{4}$". As you sew, measure your work to compare with the measurements provided, which include seam allowances, and adjust your seam allowance as needed. Arrows on diagrams indicate suggested directions to press seam allowances.

1. For **Large Square-in-a-Square**, select **square A** and 4 matching **triangles B**.

2. Sew 1 **triangle B** to 2 opposite sides of **square A** (**Fig. 1**). Sew remaining **triangles B** to square A to make **Large Square-in-a-Square**. Trim Large Square-in-a-Square to $10^1/2$" x $10^1/2$".

Fig. 1

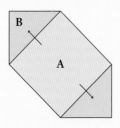

Large Square-in-a-Square

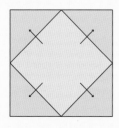

3. For 4 matching **Large Hourglasses**, select 2 **squares C** and 2 **squares D**.
4. Draw a diagonal line (corner to corner) on wrong side of each square C.
5. Matching right sides, place 1 **square C** on top of **square D**. Stitch $1/4$" from each side of drawn line (**Fig. 2**). Cut along drawn line and press seam allowances to darker fabric to make 2 **Triangle-Squares**. Triangle-Square should measure $10^7/8$" x $10^7/8$". Make 4 Triangle-Squares.

Fig. 2

Triangle-Square
(make 4)

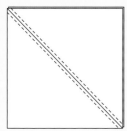
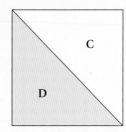

6. On wrong side of 2 Triangle-Squares, draw a diagonal line (corner to corner and perpendicular to seam).
7. Matching right sides and seams and with like fabric opposite, place 1 marked Triangle-Square on top of 1 unmarked Triangle-Square. Stitch $1/4$" from each side of drawn line (**Fig. 3**). Cut apart along drawn line and press seam allowances to one side to make 2 **Large Hourglasses**. Large Hourglass should measure $10^1/2$" x $10^1/2$". Make 4 Large Hourglasses.

Fig. 3

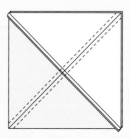

Large Hourglass (make 4)

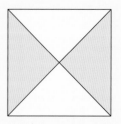

8. Trim 2" from each **Hourglass** *on the same cream print triangle side* (**Fig. 4**). Trimmed **Hourglass** should measure $10^1/2$" x $8^1/2$".

Fig. 4

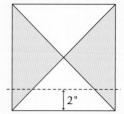

9. For 4 matching **Sawtooth Blocks**, select 4 **squares I** and 12 **squares G** from 1 print, 2 matching **squares E**, 2 matching **squares F**, and 3 sets of 4 matching **squares H**.

10. In the same manner as before and using **squares E** and **squares F**, make 4 **Very Large Triangle-Squares**. Very Large Triangle-Square should measure 6½" x 6½".

Very Large Triangle-Square (make 4)

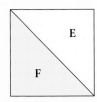

11. In the same manner as before and using **squares G** and **squares H**, make 3 sets of 8 matching **Small Triangle-Squares**. Small Triangle-Square should measure 2½" x 2½".

Small Triangle-Square
(make 3 sets of 8 matching)

12. Sew 3 non-matching **Small Triangle-Squares** and 1 **square I** together to make **Unit 1**. Unit 1 should measure 8½" x 2½". Make 4 Unit 1's.

Unit 1 (make 4)

13. Sew 3 non-matching **Small Triangle-Squares** together to make **Unit 2**. Unit 2 should measure 6½" x 2½". Make 4 Unit 2's.

Unit 2 (make 4)

14. Sew 1 **Very Large Triangle-Square** and 1 **Unit 2** together to make **Unit 3**. Make 4 Unit 3's.

Unit 3 (make 4)

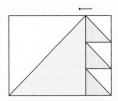

15. Sew 1 **Unit 1** and 1 **Unit 3** together to make **Sawtooth Block**. Sawtooth Block should measure 8½" x 8½". Make 4 Sawtooth Blocks.

Sawtooth Block (make 4)

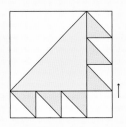

16. Sew 2 **Sawtooth Blocks** and 1 **Large Hourglass** together to make **Unit 4**. Unit 4 should measure 26½" x 8½". Make 2 Unit 4's.

Unit 4 (make 2)

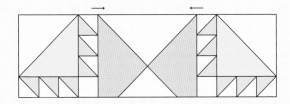

17. Sew 2 **Large Hourglasses** and **Large Square-in-a-Square** together to make **Unit 5**. Unit 5 should measure 26½" x 10½".

Unit 5

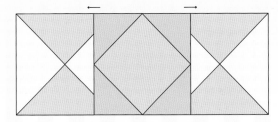

18. Sew 2 **Unit 4's** and **Unit 5** together to make **Star Center**. Star Center should measure 26^1/$_2$" x 26^1/$_2$".

Star Center

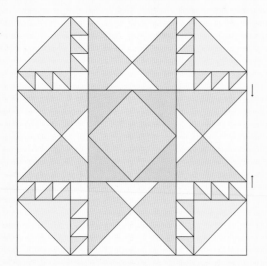

ADDING THE 1ST BORDER

1. For **1st border**, select 56 **squares J**.
2. Sew 13 **squares J** together to make **side 1st border**. Press seam allowances in one direction. Side 1st border should measure 2^1/$_2$" x 26^1/$_2$". Make 2 side 1st borders.

Side 1st Border (make 2)

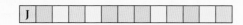

3. Matching centers and corners, sew side 1st borders to Star Center. Press seam allowances to borders.
4. Sew 15 **squares J** together to make **top 1st border**. Press seam allowances in one direction. Top 1st border should measure 2^1/$_2$" x 30^1/$_2$". Repeat to make **bottom 1st border**.

Top/Bottom 1st Border (make 2)

5. Matching centers and corners, sew top/bottom 1st borders to Star Center. Press seam allowances to borders. Quilt top should now measure 30^1/$_2$" x 30^1/$_2$".

ADDING THE 2ND BORDER

1. For **2nd border**, select 20 **squares K**, 20 **squares L**, 2 **squares M**, and 2 **squares N**.
2. In the same manner as before and using **squares K** and **squares L**, make 40 **Small Hourglasses**. Small Hourglass should measure 3^1/$_2$" x 3^1/$_2$".

Small Hourglass (make 40)

3. In the same manner as before and using **squares M** and **squares N**, make 4 **Medium Triangle-Squares**. Medium Triangle-Square should measure 3^1/$_2$" x 3^1/$_2$".

Medium Triangle-Square (make 4)

4. Sew 10 **Small Hourglasses** together to make **side 2nd border**. Press seam allowances open or in one direction. Side 2nd border should measure 3^1/$_2$" x 30^1/$_2$". Make 2 side 2nd borders.

Side 2nd Border (make 2)

5. Sew 2 **Medium Triangle-Squares** and 10 **Small Hourglasses** together to make **top 2nd border**. Press seam allowances open or to the Triangle-Squares. Top 2nd border should measure $3^{1}/_{2}$" x $36^{1}/_{2}$" Repeat to make **bottom 2nd border**.

Top/Bottom 2nd Border (make 2)

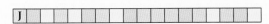

6. In the same manner as 1st border, sew side and then top/bottom 2nd borders to quilt top. Press seam allowances to 1st border. Quilt top should now measure $36^{1}/_{2}$" x $36^{1}/_{2}$".

ADDING THE 3RD BORDER

1. For **3rd border**, select 76 **squares J**.
2. Sew 18 **squares J** together to make **side 3rd border**. Press seam allowances in one direction. Side 3rd border should measure $2^{1}/_{2}$" x $36^{1}/_{2}$". Make 2 side 3rd borders.

Side 3rd Border (make 2)

3. Sew 20 **squares J** together to make **top 1st border**. Press seam allowances in one direction. Top 1st border should measure $2^{1}/_{2}$" x $40^{1}/_{2}$". Repeat to make **bottom 3rd border**.

Top/Bottom 3rd Border (make 2)

4. In the same manner as 1st border, sew side and then top/bottom 3rd borders to quilt top. Press seam allowances to 3rd border. Quilt top should now measure $40^{1}/_{2}$" x $40^{1}/_{2}$".

ADDING THE 4TH BORDER

1. For **4th border**, select 44 **squares O**.
2. In the same manner as before and using **squares O**, make 44 **Large Triangle-Squares**. Large Triangle-Square should measure $4^{1}/_{2}$" x $4^{1}/_{2}$".

Large Triangle-Square (make 44)

3. Sew 10 **Large Triangle-Squares** together to make **side 4th border**. Press seam allowances open or in one direction. Side 4th border should measure $4^{1}/_{2}$" x $40^{1}/_{2}$". Make 2 side 4th borders.

Side 4th Border (make 2)

4. Sew 12 **Large Triangle-Squares** together to make **top 4th border**. Press seam allowances open or in one direction. Top 4th border should measure $4^{1}/_{2}$" x $48^{1}/_{2}$" Repeat to make **bottom 4th border**.

Top/Bottom 4th Border (make 2)

5. In the same manner as 1st border, sew side and then top/bottom 4th borders to quilt top. Press seam allowances to 4th border. Quilt top should now measure $48^{1}/_{2}$" x $48^{1}/_{2}$".

MAKING THE STAR BLOCKS

1. For **Star Block**, select 1 **square R**, 1 **square P**, 4 matching **squares Q**, and 4 matching **squares I**.
2. Draw a diagonal line (corner to corner) on wrong side of each **square Q**.
3. Matching right sides, place 1 **square Q** on opposite corners of **square P** (**Fig. 5**); pin in place.

Fig. 5

4. Stitch $1/4$" from each side of drawn lines (**Fig. 6**). Cut along drawn lines to make 2 **Unit 6's**.

Fig. 6

Unit 6 (make 2)

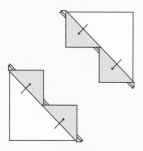

5. Matching corners, place 1 **square Q** on each **Unit 6** (**Fig. 7**).

Fig. 7

6. Stitch seam $1/4$" from each side of drawn lines (**Fig. 8**). Cut along drawn lines to make 4 **Flying Geese A's**. Flying Geese A should measure $4^{1}/_{2}$" x $2^{1}/_{2}$".

Fig. 8

Flying Geese A (make 4)

7. Sew 2 **squares I** and 1 **Flying Geese A** together to make **Unit 7**. Make 2 Unit 7's.

Unit 7 (make 2)

8. Sew 2 **Flying Geese A's** and 1 **square R** together to make **Unit 8**.

Unit 8

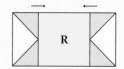

9. Sew 2 **Unit 7's** and **Unit 8** together to make **Star Block**. Star Block should measure $8^{1}/_{2}$" x $8^{1}/_{2}$".
10. Repeat **Steps 1–9** to make 24 Star Blocks.

Star Block (make 24)

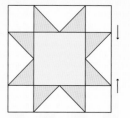

MAKING THE CORNER BLOCKS

. For **Corner Block**, select 2 matching **squares G**, 4 matching **squares G**, 2 matching **squares H**, 4 matching **squares I**, 1 **square S**, and 1 **square T**.

. Draw a diagonal line (corner to corner) on wrong side of each **square G** and each **square I**.

. With right sides together, place 1 **square I** on 1 corner of **square T** and stitch diagonally (**Fig. 9**). Trim ¹/₄" from stitching line (**Fig. 10**). Open up and press (**Fig. 11**).

Fig. 9   Fig. 10

Fig. 11

. Continue adding **squares I** to square T to make **Small Square-in-a-Square**. Small Square-in-a-Square should measure 4¹/₂" x 4¹/₂".

Small Square-in-a-Square

. In the same manner as before and using 2 matching **squares G** and 2 matching **squares H**, make 4 **Small Triangle-Squares**. Small Triangle-Square should measure 2¹/₂" x 2¹/₂".

Small Triangle-Square (make 4)

6. In the same manner as before and using 4 matching **squares G** and **square S**, make 4 **Flying Geese B's**. Flying Geese B should measure 4¹/₂" x 2¹/₄".

Flying Geese B (make 4)

7. Sew 2 **Small Triangle-Squares** and 1 **Flying Geese B** together to make **Unit 9**. Make 2 Unit 9's.

Unit 9 (make 2)

8. Sew 2 **Flying Geese B's** and 1 **Small Square-in-a-Square** together to make **Unit 10**.

Unit 10

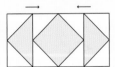

9. Sew 2 **Unit 9's** and **Unit 10** together to make **Corner Block**. Corner Block should measure 8¹/₂" x 8¹/₂".

10. Repeat **Steps 1–9** to make 4 Corner Blocks.

Corner Block (make 4)

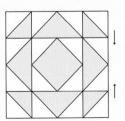

ADDING THE 5TH BORDER

1. Sew 6 **Star Blocks** together to make **side 5th border**. Press seam allowances open or in one direction. Side 5th border should measure $8^1/2$" x $48^1/2$". Make 2 side 5th borders.

Side 5th Border (make 2)

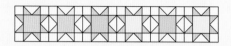

2. Sew 2 **Corner Blocks** and 6 **Star Blocks** together to make **top 5th border**. Press seam allowances open or in one direction. Top 5th border should measure $8^1/2$" x $64^1/2$". Repeat to make **bottom 5th border**.

Top/Bottom 5th Border (make 2)

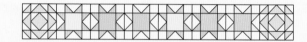

3. In the same manner as 1st border, sew side and then top/bottom 5th borders to quilt top. Press seam allowances to 4th border. Quilt top should now measure $64^1/2$" x $64^1/2$".

ADDING THE 6TH BORDER

1. Sew 4 **rectangles U** and 8 **rectangles V** together to make **side 6th border**. Press seam allowances in one direction. Make 2 side 6th borders.

Side 6th Border (make 2)

2. Measure *length* across center of quilt top and length of side 6th borders. If measurements are not the same, make seams in borders slightly larger or smaller as needed.

3. Sew 2 **squares W**, 4 **rectangles U**, and 8 **rectangles V** together to make **top 6th border**. Press seam allowances in one direction. Repeat to make **bottom 6th border**.

Top/Bottom 6th Border (make 2)

4. Measure *width* across center of quilt top (including added borders) and length of top/bottom 6th borders. If measurements are not the same, make seams in borders slightly larger or smaller as needed.

5. In the same manner as 1st border, sew side and then top/bottom 6th borders to quilt top. Press seam allowances to 6th border. Quilt top should measure $76^1/2$" x $76^1/2$".

COMPLETING THE QUILT

1. To help stabilize the edges and prevent any seams from separating, stay-stitch around the quilt top approximately $1/8$" from the edge.

2. Follow **Machine Quilting**, page 107, to mark, layer, and quilt as desired. Quilt shown was machine quilted. The cream areas were stipple quilted. The pastel areas were quilted with a combination of straight-line patterns, curving patterns, and feather patterns.

3. Follow **Making a Hanging Sleeve**, page 109, if a hanging sleeve is desired.

4. Cut a 27" square of binding fabric. Follow **Binding**, page 109, to bind quilt using 2"w bias binding with mitered corners.

NOTE: The easiest way to make this quilt larger is to add a plain border. The rectangles in the 6th border can be cut a different width—either wider for a larger quilt or narrower for a smaller quilt.

Assembly Diagram

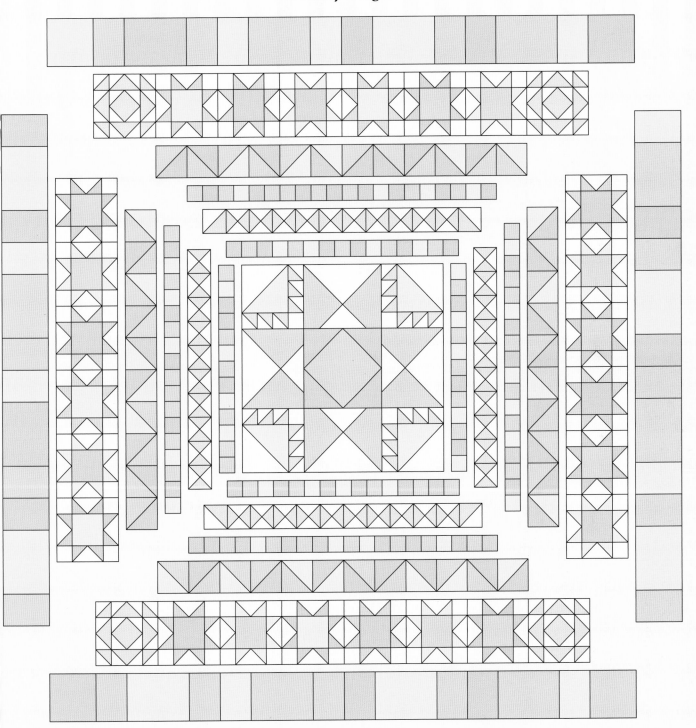

Don't be CRUEL

Quilted by Louise Haley.

Finished Quilt Size:
66¹/₂" x 74¹/₂" (169 cm x 189 cm)

Do you remember? Back in the day of 45 RPM records, each record had a Side A and a Side B. Each side had only one song. This quilt and the one on page 40—"Hound Dog"—are named for the A and B sides of an Elvis Presley record. By the way, that particular record was one of the few instances where both sides became a Number One hit song.

Although the construction method for "Don't Be Cruel" and "Hound Dog" are basically the same, you will end up with two very different "songs" to play.

Yardage Requirements

Yardage is based on 43"/44" (109 cm/112 cm) wide fabric. Fat quarters are approximately 21" x 18" (53 cm x 46 cm). Fat eighths are approximately 21" x 9" (53 cm x 23 cm). Jelly Rolls contain strips that are approximately $2^1/2$" x 42" (6 cm x 107 cm).

- 23 fat quarters *or* 54 fat eighths *or* 2 Jelly Rolls (a total of 80 strips) of assorted light, medium, and dark print fabrics
- $3/8$ yd (34 cm) of fabric for inner border
- $7/8$ yd (80 cm) of fabric for binding
- $4^5/8$ yds (4.2 m) of fabric for backing

You will also need:

- 75" x 83" (191 cm x 211 cm) piece of batting

Cutting Out the Pieces

*Follow **Rotary Cutting**, page 105, to cut fabric. All measurements include $1/4$" seam allowances.*

If using fat quarters:
- Cut 7 **strips** $2^1/2$" x 21" from *each* fat quarter. Cut a total of 160 strips.

If using fat eighths:
- Cut 3 **strips** $2^1/2$" x 21" from *each* fat eighth. Cut a total of 160 strips.

If using jelly rolls:
- Cut *each* strip in half to make 2 **strips** $2^1/2$" x 21". Cut a total of 160 strips.

From fabric for inner border:
- Cut 8 **inner border strips** $1^1/2$" x the width of the fabric.

Assembling the Panels

The quilt top center is constructed of 4 Panels. Each of the 4 Panels is made using a group of strips. While the groups may have some strips of the same fabrics, the placement of the strips is random so each Panel will be different.

*Follow **Piecing**, page 106, and **Pressing**, page 107, to assemble quilt top. Because there are so many seams in this quilt, you may need to use a seam allowance slightly smaller than the usual $1/4$". As you sew, measure your work to compare with the measurements provided, which include seam allowances, and adjust your seam allowance as needed. Arrows on diagrams indicate directions to press seam allowances.*

1. With as much variety in each group as possible, divide the **strips** into 4 groups of 40 strips each.

Panel A's

1. Select 1 group of strips. Divide this group into 4 sub-groups of 8 strips. Set aside the remaining 8 strips for the border.
2. Using 1 sub-group, sew the strips together in random order to make **Strip Set**. *Do not* press seam allowances yet. Make 4 Strip Sets of 8 strips each.

Strip Set

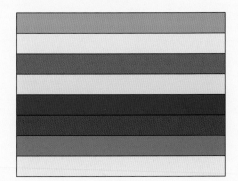

. For **Panel A**, lay out Strip Sets in desired order from top to bottom. Using a piece of masking tape or an adhesive label, label the top strip on each Strip Set in numerical order (**Fig. 1**). Press seam allowances to **even**-number strips. Strip Set should measure 21" x 16^1/$_2$".

Fig. 1

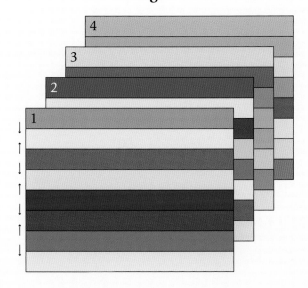

4. Beginning with **Strip Set #4** (the Strip Set that will be at the bottom of the panel), cut across Strip Set at 2^1/$_2$" intervals to make 8 **Unit 1's**. Unit 1 should measure 2^1/$_2$" x 16^1/$_2$". As you cut each Unit, place it in separate stack (#1–#8). If you can cut 9 Unit 1's from the Strip Set, do so, even if some of the strips in the Unit are not complete. Set aside these Unit 1's and partial Unit 1's in stack #9.

Unit 1

5. Continuing with **Strip Set #3** and ending with **Strip Set #1**, repeat **Step 4** for each Strip Set. As you cut Units, work in same order as previously and place 1 Unit on each stack. Each stack will have one Unit 1 from each Strip Set and the Unit 1's will be in the order they will need to be sewn.
6. Keeping the stacks separate, set aside stack #8 and stack #9 for border.
7. Using stack #1, sew Unit 1's together in order to make vertical **Row 1**. Press seam allowances between Unit 1's so that they continue the same alternating pattern from the Unit 1's. Row 1 should measure 2^1/$_2$" x 64^1/$_2$". Label Row 1.
8. Working in order, repeat **Step 7** to make vertical **Rows 2–7**; label each Row. Each Row should measure 2^1/$_2$" x 64^1/$_2$".

9. Referring to **Fig. 2** and following list below, use a seam ripper to remove squares from top of Rows and sew them to bottom of Rows.
   - Row 2 – remove the top square and sew it to the bottom of the Row.
   - Row 3 – remove the top 2 squares and sew them to the bottom of the Row.
   - Row 4 – remove the top 3 squares and sew them to the bottom of the Row.
   - Row 5 – remove the top 4 squares and sew them to the bottom of the Row.
   - Row 6 – remove the top 5 squares and sew them to the bottom of the Row.
   - Row 7 – remove the top 6 squares and sew them to the bottom of the Row.

10. To complete **Panel A**, keep Rows in numerical order, align short ends, and match long edges to sew Rows together. If everything is pressed correctly, all the seam allowances should be opposing each other. Press long seam allowances in one direction. Panel A should measure $14^1/_2$" x $64^1/_2$".

11. Repeat **Steps 1–10**, to make a second Panel A.

Panel B's

1. For **Panel B**, follow **Panel A's**, **Steps 1–2**, to make 4 **Strip Sets**, setting aside 8 strips for border. Pressing seam allowances to **odd**-number strips (**Fig. 3**), follow **Panel A's**, **Step 3**, to order and label Strip Sets.

Fig. 2

Fig. 3

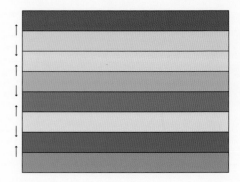

2. Follow **Panel A's**, **Steps 4–8**, to make and label 7 vertical **Rows**.

3. Referring to **Fig. 4** and following list below, use a seam ripper to remove squares from bottom of Rows and sew them to top of Rows.
   - Row 2 – remove the bottom square and sew it to the top of the Row.
   - Row 3 – remove the bottom 2 squares and sew them to the top of the Row.
   - Row 4 – remove the bottom 3 squares and sew them to the top of the Row.
   - Row 5 – remove the bottom 4 squares and sew them to the top of the Row.
   - Row 6 – remove the bottom 5 squares and sew them to the top of the Row.
   - Row 7 – remove the bottom 6 squares and sew them to the top of the Row.

Fig. 4

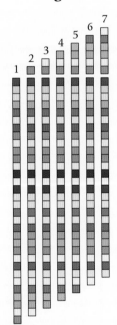

4. Follow **Panel A's, Step 10**, to complete **Panel B**. Press long seam allowances in one direction. Panel B should measure $14^{1}/_{2}$" x $64^{1}/_{2}$".
5. Follow **Panel B's, Steps 1–4**, to make a second Panel B.

ASSEMBLING THE QUILT TOP CENTER
Refer to Assembly Diagram, page 39, for placement.
1. Alternating panels, sew **Panel A's** and **B's** together to make quilt top center. Press seam allowances in one direction. Quilt top center should measure $56^{1}/_{2}$" x $64^{1}/_{2}$".

ADDING THE INNER BORDER
1. Using diagonal seams (**Fig. 5**), sew 2 **inner border strips** together to make **inner border**. Make 4 inner borders. Press seam allowances open.

Fig. 5

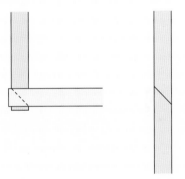

2. Measure *length* across center of quilt top center. Trim 2 inner borders to determined length to make **side inner borders**. Matching centers and corners, sew side inner borders to quilt top center. Press seam allowances to inner border.
3. Measure *width* across center of quilt top center (including added borders). Trim remaining inner borders to determined length to make **top/bottom inner borders**. Matching centers and corners, sew top/bottom inner borders to quilt top center. Press seam allowances to inner border.

ADDING THE OUTER BORDER
To piece the outer border you will need 264 squares $2^{1}/_{2}$" x $2^{1}/_{2}$". The squares will come from 3 different sources: the stack #8's of Unit 1's, the stack #9's of Unit 1's or squares, and the strips set aside earlier.
1. Divide the strips set aside for the outer borders into 8 groups of 4 strips each.

2. Using 1 group of 4, sew the strips together in random order to make **Strip Set**. Strip Set should measure 21" x 8$^1/_2$". Press seam allowances in one direction. Make 8 Strip Sets.

Strip Set (make 8)

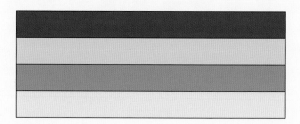

3. Cut across Strip Sets at 2$^1/_2$" intervals to make 32 **Unit 2's**. Unit 2 should measure 2$^1/_2$" x 8$^1/_2$".

Unit 2 (make 32)

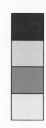

4. Using Unit 2's, Unit 1's from stack #8's, and Unit 1's or squares from stack #9's, make 1 **Border Unit** containing 33 squares. Press seam allowances in one direction. Cutting additional Unit 2's as needed, make a total of 8 Border Units.
5. Matching long edges, sew 2 **Border Units** together to make **outer border**. Press seam allowances to one side. Make 4 outer borders.

6. Measure *length* across center of quilt top. Measure length of 2 outer borders. If measurements are not the same, make seam allowances in borders slightly larger or smaller as needed for **side outer borders**. Matching centers and corners, sew side outer borders to quilt top. Press seam allowances to outer border.
7. Measure *width* across center of quilt top (including added borders). Measure length of remaining outer borders. If measurements are not the same, make seam allowances in borders slightly larger or smaller as needed for **top/bottom outer borders**. Matching centers and corners, sew top/bottom borders to quilt top. Press seam allowances to outer border. Quilt top should measure 66$^1/_2$" x 74$^1/_2$".

COMPLETING THE QUILT

1. To help stabilize the edges and prevent any seams from separating, stay-stitch around quilt top approximately $^1/_8$" from the edge.
2. Follow **Machine Quilting**, page 107, to mark, layer, and quilt as desired. Quilt shown was machine quilted in the ditch along the inner border. A curved line pattern was quilted in each square. A loop pattern was quilted in the inner border.
3. Follow **Making a Hanging Sleeve**, page 109, if a hanging sleeve is desired.
4. Cut a 26" square of binding fabric. Follow **Binding**, page 109, to bind quilt using 2"w bias binding with mitered corners.

NOTE: This quilt can be made longer or shorter by adding or subtracting strips to the Strip Sets. Adding or subtracting 1 strip to each Strip Set will change the finished length of the quilt by 8". The quilt can also be made larger by adding a plain border.

Assembly Diagram

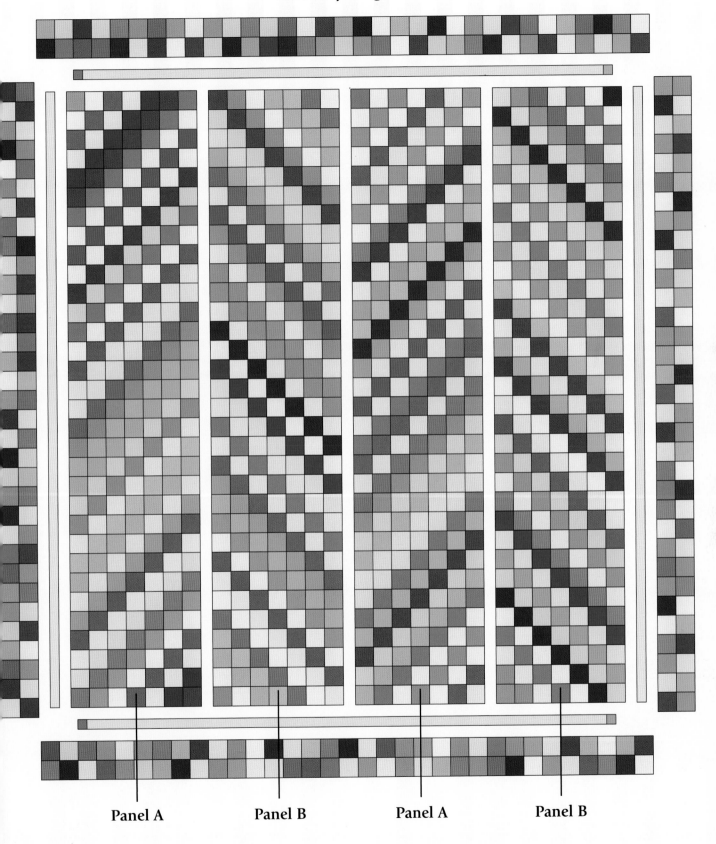

Panel A   Panel B   Panel A   Panel B

Hound DOG

Quilted by Diane Tricka.

Finished Quilt Size:
74^1/$_2$" x 82^1/$_2$" (189 cm x 210 cm)

This quilt uses lots of rectangles and a few triangles, giving it a lively sort of tempo, just like the song of the same name. The repeated squares or rectangles of "Don't Be Cruel" (page 32) and "Hound Dog" are some of my favorite themes.

Over the years, I've used strips swapped with friends to make similar quilts. I've made them using fat quarters, homespun plaids, reproduction fabrics, and stuff from my scrap bag. The piecing is simple, and this is a great way to practice your seam allowance and pressing techniques!

YARDAGE REQUIREMENTS

Yardage is based on 43"/44" (109 cm/112 cm) wide fabric. Fat quarters are approximately 21" x 18" (53 cm x 46 cm). Fat eighths are approximately 21" x 9" (53 cm x 23 cm). Jelly Rolls contain strips that are approximately 2¹/₂" x 42" (6 cm x 107 cm). Charm packs contain squares that are approximately 5" x 5" (13 cm x 13 cm).

- 21 fat quarters *or* 48 fat eighths *or* 2 Jelly Rolls (a total of 72 strips) of assorted light, medium, and dark print fabrics
- 1 or 2 charm packs (a total of 40 squares) for outer border
- ⁵/₈ yd (57 cm) of assorted tan print fabrics for inner border
- ⁷/₈ yd (80 cm) of fabric for binding
- 7 yds (6.4 m) of fabric for backing

You will also need:

- 83" x 91" (211 cm x 231 cm) piece of batting

CUTTING OUT THE PIECES

*Follow **Rotary Cutting**, page 105, to cut fabric. All measurements include ¹/₄" seam allowances.*

If using fat quarters:
- Cut 7 **strips** 2¹/₂" x 21" from *each* fat quarter. Cut a total of 144 strips.

If using fat eighths:
- Cut 3 **strips** 2¹/₂" x 21" from *each* fat eighth. Cut a total of 144 strips.

If using jelly rolls:
- Cut *each* strip in half to make 2 **strips** 2¹/₂" x 21". Cut a total of 144 strips.

From assorted tan print fabrics for inner border:
- Cut a total of 32 **inner border strips** 1¹/₂" x 11".

ASSEMBLING THE PANELS

The quilt top center is constructed of 4 Panels. Each of the 4 Panels is made using a group of strips. While the groups may have some strips of the same fabrics, the placement of the strips is random so each Panel will be different.

*Follow **Piecing**, page 106, and **Pressing**, page 107, to assemble quilt top. Because there are so many seams in this quilt, you may need to use a seam allowance slightly smaller than the usual ¹/₄". As you sew, measure your work to compare with the measurements provided, which include seam allowances, and adjust your seam allowance as needed. Arrows on diagrams indicate directions to press seam allowances.*

1. With as much variety in each group as possible, divide the **strips** into 4 groups of 36 strips each.

Panel A's
1. Select 1 group of strips. Divide this group into 6 sub-groups of 6 strips.
2. Using 1 sub-group, sew the strips together in random order to make **Strip Set**. ***Do not*** press seam allowances yet. Make 6 Strip Sets of 6 strips each.

Strip Set

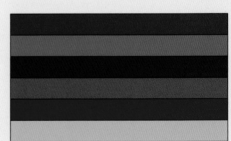

3. For **Panel A**, lay out Strip Sets in desired order from top to bottom. Using a piece of masking tape or an adhesive label, label the top strip on each Strip Set in numerical order (**Fig. 1**). Press seam allowances to **even**-number strips. Strip Set should measure 21" x 12$\frac{1}{2}$".

Fig. 1

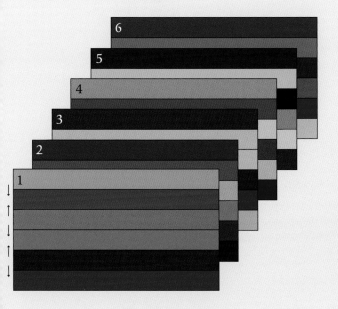

4. Beginning with **Strip Set #6** (the Strip Set that will be at the bottom of the panel), cut across Strip Set at 4$\frac{1}{2}$" intervals to make 4 **Unit 1's**. Unit 1 should measure 4$\frac{1}{2}$" x 12$\frac{1}{2}$". Cut across remainder of Strip Set at a 2$\frac{1}{2}$" interval to make **Unit 2**. Unit 2 should measure 2$\frac{1}{2}$" x 12$\frac{1}{2}$". As you cut each Unit, place it in a separate stack (#1–#5.)

Unit 1 (cut 4)   **Unit 2** (cut 1)

5. Continuing with **Strip Set #5** and ending with **Strip Set #1**, repeat **Step** 4 for each Strip Set. As you cut Units, work in same order as previously and place 1 Unit on each stack. Four stacks will contain 1 Unit 1 from each Strip Set and 1 stack will contain 1 Unit 2 from each Strip Set. The Units will be in the order they will need to be sewn. Set aside the stack of Unit 2's for border.

6. Using stack #1, sew Unit 1's together in order to make vertical **Row 1**. Press seam allowances between Unit 1's so that they continue the same alternating pattern from the Unit 1's. Row 1 should measure 4$\frac{1}{2}$" x 72$\frac{1}{2}$". Label Row 1.

7. Working in order, repeat **Step 6** to make vertical **Rows 2–4**; label each Row. Each Row should measure 4$\frac{1}{2}$" x 72$\frac{1}{2}$".

8. Referring to **Fig. 2** and following list below, use a seam ripper to remove pieces from top of Rows and sew them to bottom of Rows.
   - Row 2 – remove the top rectangle and sew it to the bottom of the Row.
   - Row 3 – remove the top 2 rectangles and sew them to the bottom of the Row.
   - Row 4 – remove the top 3 rectangles and sew them to the bottom of the Row.

Fig. 2

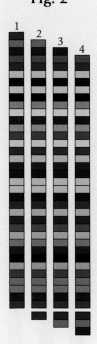

9. To complete **Panel A**, keep Rows in numerical order, align short ends, and match long edges to sew Rows together. If everything is pressed correctly, all the seam allowances should be opposing each other. Press long seam allowances in one direction. Panel A should measure $16^1/_2$" x $72^1/_2$".

10. Repeat **Steps 1–9** to make a second Panel A.

Panel B's

1. For **Panel B**, follow **Panel A's**, **Steps 1–2**, to make 6 **Strip Sets**. Pressing seam allowances to the **odd**-number strips (**Fig. 3**), follow **Panel A's**, **Step 3**, to order and label Strip Sets.

Fig. 3

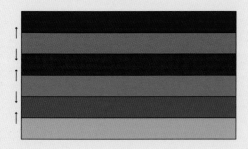

2. Follow **Panel A's**, **Steps 4-7**, to make and label 4 vertical **Rows**.

3. Referring to **Fig. 4** and following list below, use a seam ripper to remove pieces from bottom of Rows and sew them to top of Rows.
   - Row 2 – remove the bottom rectangle and sew it to the top of the Row.
   - Row 3 – remove the bottom 2 rectangles and sew them to the top of the Row.
   - Row 4 – remove the bottom 3 rectangles and sew them to the top of the Row.

Fig. 4

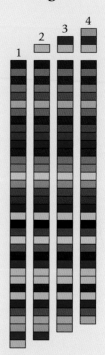

4. Follow **Panel A**, **Step 9**, to complete **Panel B**. Panel B should measure $16^1/_2$" x $72^1/_2$".

5. Follow **Panel B**, **Steps 1–4** to make a second Panel B.

ASSEMBLING THE QUILT TOP CENTER
*Refer to **Assembly Diagram**, page 47, for placement.*

1. Alternating panels, sew **Panel A's** and **B's** together to make quilt top center. Press seam allowances in one direction. Quilt top center should measure $64^1/_2$" x $72^1/_2$".

ADDING THE INNER BORDER

1. Using diagonal seams (**Fig. 5**), sew 8 **inner border strips** together to make **inner border**. Press seam allowances open. Make 4 inner borders.

Fig. 5

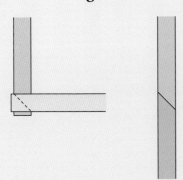

2. Measure *length* across center of quilt top center. Trim 2 inner borders to determined length to make **side inner borders**. Matching centers and corners, sew side inner borders to quilt top center. Press seam allowances to inner border.

3. Measure *width* across center of quilt top center (including added borders). Trim remaining inner borders to determined length to make **top/bottom inner borders**. Matching centers and corners, sew top/bottom inner borders to quilt top center. Press seam allowances to inner border.

ADDING THE OUTER BORDER

To piece the outer border you will need 24 Unit 2's and 40 charm squares 5" x 5" (13 cm x 13 cm).

1. Sort the **charm squares** into 20 pairs of squares.

2. Draw a diagonal line on wrong side of 1 charm square from each pair. With right sides together, place marked charm square on top of unmarked charm square from pair. Stitch seam $1/4$" from each side of drawn line (**Fig. 6**).

Fig. 6

3. Cut along drawn line and press seam allowances to darker fabric to make 2 **Triangle-Squares**. Trim each Triangle-Square to $4^1/2$" x $4^1/2$". Make 40 Triangle-Squares.

Triangle-Square (make 40)

4. Sew 10 **Triangle-Squares** together in a random pattern to make **Unit 3**. Press seam allowances open or in one direction. Unit 3 should measure $4^1/2$" x $40^1/2$". Make 4 Unit 3's.

Unit 3 (make 4)

5. Sew 3 **Unit 2's** together and then remove 1 square to make **Unit 4**. Press seam allowances in one direction. Unit 4 should measure $2^1/2$" x $34^1/2$". Make 8 Unit 4's.

Unit 4 (make 8)

45

6. Sew 2 **Unit 4's** together to make **Unit 5**. Press seam allowances to one side. Unit 5 should measure $4^1/_2$" x $34^1/_2$". Make 4 Unit 5's.

Unit 5 (make 4)

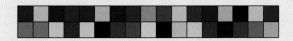

7. Sew 1 **Unit 3** and 1 **Unit 5** together to make **outer border**. Press seam allowances to one side. Make 4 outer borders.

Outer Border (make 4)

8. Measure *length* across center of quilt top. Measure length of 2 outer borders. If measurements are not the same, make seam allowances in borders slightly larger or smaller as needed for **side outer borders**. Matching centers and corners, sew side outer borders to quilt top. Press seam allowances to outer border.

9. Measure *width* across center of quilt top (including added borders). Measure length of remaining outer borders. If measurements are not the same, make seam allowances in borders slightly larger or smaller as needed for **top/bottom outer borders**. Matching centers and corners, sew top/bottom outer borders to quilt top. Press seam allowances to outer border. Quilt top should measure $74^1/_2$" x $82^1/_2$".

COMPLETING THE QUILT

1. To help stabilize the edges and prevent any seams from separating, stay-stitch around the quilt top approximately $^1/_8$" from the edge.
2. Follow **Machine Quilting**, page 107, to mark, layer, and quilt as desired. Quilt shown was machine quilted. Horizontal and vertical lines were alternated in the rectangles. A flower was quilted in each square and Triangle-Square of the outer border. The inner border was quilted in the ditch and with a continuous leaf pattern.
3. Follow **Making a Hanging Sleeve**, page 109, if a hanging sleeve is desired.
4. Cut a 28" square of binding fabric. Follow **Binding**, page 109, to bind quilt using 2"w bias binding with mitered corners.

NOTE: This quilt can be made longer or shorter by adding or subtracting strips to the Strip Sets. Adding or subtracting a strip to each Strip Set will change the finished length of the quilt by 12". Or, a plain border may be added to make the quilt larger.

Panel A   Panel B   Panel A   Panel B

Luci in THE SKY

Quilted by Louise Haley.

Finished Quilt Size:
72³/₈" x 84¹/₂" (184 cm x 215 cm)
Finished Block Size:
11³/₈" x 11³/₈" (29 cm x 29 cm)

I want to assure you that you will not have to sew any set-in seams for the stars on this quilt! They only look like they have set-in seams because of a neat little cutting technique. And that came about because I don't like templates. Truth be told, I avoid them like the plague. So I had this idea. Instead of making a pieced unit that would require three different templates, I made something we all know how to make—an Hourglass—and I lopped off a little bit on one side. Same result. Much easier process!

This quilt is another one that will work well with any style of fabric, whether it's dark or light, floral or plaid, high or low contrast, a dozen different fabrics or ten dozen.

As for the name of this quilt, it comes partly from the fabric collection, which used the name "Luci," and partly from the famous song about another Lucy in the sky. This quilted Luci is in the sky with stars instead of diamonds.

Yardage Requirements

Yardage is based on 43"/44" (109 cm/112 cm) wide fabric. Fat quarters are approximately 21" x 18" (53 cm x 46 cm).

- 12 fat quarters of assorted light (tan) print fabrics
- 24 fat quarters of assorted dark (blue, red, pink, and black) print fabrics
- $5/8$ yd (57 cm) of green print fabric
- $7/8$ yd (80 cm) of fabric for binding
- $6^3/4$ yds (6.2 m)* of fabric for backing

You will also need:

- 81" x 93" (206 cm x 236 cm) piece of batting

*Yardage is based on three 81" (206 cm) lengths of fabric, which allows for a larger backing for long arm quilting. If you are using another quilting method, two 93" (236 cm) lengths or $5^1/4$ yds (4.8 m), will be adequate.

Cutting Out the Pieces

*Follow **Rotary Cutting**, page 105, to cut fabric. All measurements include $1/4$" seam allowances. Triangles are slightly larger than needed and will be trimmed.*

From *each* of 6 assorted light print fat quarters:
- Cut 1 strip $6^7/8$" x 21". From this strip,
  - Cut 2 **large squares** $6^7/8$" x $6^7/8$". Cut a total of 12 large squares.
- Cut 1 strip $4^1/4$" x 21". From this strip,
  - Cut 3 **medium squares** $4^1/4$" x $4^1/4$". Cut a total of 18 medium squares.
- Cut 2 strips 3" x 21". From these strips,
  - Cut 12 **small squares** 3" x 3". Cut a total of 72 small squares.

Set remaining scraps aside.

From *each* of remaining 6 assorted light print fat quarters:
- Cut 1 strip $6^7/8$" x 21". From this strip,
  - Cut 2 **large squares** $6^7/8$" x $6^7/8$". Cut a total of 12 large squares. You will have 24 large squares.
- Cut 1 strip $4^1/4$" x 21". From this strip,
  - Cut 2 **medium squares** $4^1/4$" x $4^1/4$". Cut a total of 12 medium squares. You will have 30 medium squares.
- Cut 2 strips 3" x 21". From these strips,
  - Cut 8 **small squares** 3" x 3". Cut a total of 48 small squares. You will have 120 (30 sets of 4 matching) small squares.

Set remaining scraps aside.

From *each* assorted dark print fat quarter:
- Cut 1 strip $6^3/4$" x 21". From this strip,
  - Cut 3 squares $6^3/4$" x $6^3/4$". Cut a total of 60 squares. Cut squares *once* diagonally to make 120 **triangles**.
- Cut 1 strip $4^1/4$" x 21". From this strip,
  - Cut 2 or 4 **medium squares** $4^1/4$" x $4^1/4$". Cut a total of 60 (30 sets of 2 matching medium squares).
- Cut 1 **large square** $6^7/8$" x $6^7/8$". Cut a total of 24 large squares.

Set remaining scraps aside.

From green print fabric:
- Cut 4 **side border strips** 2" x the width of the fabric.
- Cut 4 **top/bottom border strips** $2^3/8$" x the width of the fabric. *(Notice that top/bottom border strips are wider than side border strips.)*

Set remaining scraps aside.

From remaining scraps set aside:
- Cut a total of 30 assorted **accent squares** $4^1/4$" x $4^1/4$".
- Cut a total of 30 assorted **center squares** $3^1/2$" x $3^1/2$".

Again, set remaining scraps aside.

Making the Hourglasses

*Follow **Piecing**, page 106, and **Pressing**, page 107, to assemble quilt top. Because there are so many seams in this quilt, you may need to use a seam allowance slightly smaller than the usual $1/4$". As you sew, measure your work to compare with the measurements provided, which include seam allowances, and adjust your seam allowance as needed. Arrows on diagrams indicate suggested directions to press seam allowances.*

1. For 4 matching **Hourglasses**, select 2 matching dark **medium squares**, 1 light **medium square**, and 1 **accent square**.

2. Draw a diagonal line (corner to corner) on wrong side of **accent square** and light **medium square**.

3. Matching right sides, place **accent square** on top of 1 dark **medium square**. Stitch $1/4$" from each side of drawn line (**Fig. 1**). Cut along drawn line and press seam allowances to dark fabric to make 2 **Triangle-Square A's**. Triangle-Square A should measure $3^7/8$" x $3^7/8$".

Fig. 1

Triangle-Square A (make 2)

4. Using light **medium square** and remaining dark **medium square**, make 2 **Triangle-Square B's**. Triangle-Square B should measure $3^7/8$" x $3^7/8$".

Triangle-Square B (make 2)

5. On wrong side of each Triangle-Square A, draw a diagonal line (corner to corner and perpendicular to seam).

6. Matching right sides and seams and with like fabrics opposite, place 1 Triangle-Square A on top of 1 Triangle-Square B. Stitch $1/4$" from each side of drawn line (**Fig. 2**). Cut apart along drawn line and press seam allowances to side with accent fabric to make 2 **Hourglasses**. Hourglass should measure $3^1/2$" x $3^1/2$". Make 4 matching Hourglasses.

Fig. 2

7. Repeat **Steps 1–6** to make 30 sets of 4 matching Hourglasses.

Hourglass
(make 30 sets of 4 matching)

8. Trim $1/2$" from each **Hourglass** *on accent triangle side* (**Fig. 3**). Trimmed **Hourglass** should now measure $3^1/2$" x 3".

Fig. 3

Making the Blocks

1. For **Block**, select 4 assorted **triangles**, 4 matching **Hourglasses**, 4 matching **small squares** (the same fabric print as the light print in the Hourglasses), and 1 **center square**.

2. Some of the center squares in quilt shown are **Snowballs**. You may add as many Snowballs as you wish. For Snowball, follow **Steps 3–5**. If not making Snowball, skip to **Step 6**.

3. Choose fabric scrap (from remaining scraps set aside earlier) of same print as accent portion of Hourglasses. From this scrap, cut 4 **very small squares** 1" x 1".

4. With right sides together, place 1 **very small square** on 1 corner of **center square** and stitch diagonally (**Fig. 4**). Trim $1/4$" from stitching line (**Fig. 5**). Open up and press (**Fig. 6**).

Fig. 4

Fig. 5

Fig. 6

5. Continue adding **very small squares** to center square to make **Snowball**. Snowball should measure $3^1/2$" x $3^1/2$".

Snowball

6. Sew 2 **small squares** and 1 **Hourglass** together to make **Unit 1**. Make 2 Unit 1's.

Unit 1 (make 2)

7. Sew 2 **Hourglasses** and **center square** *or* **Snowball** together to make **Unit 2**.

Unit 2

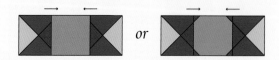

or

8. Sew 2 **Unit 1's** and **Unit 2** together to make **Star Unit**. Star Unit should measure $8^1/2$" x $8^1/2$".

Star Unit

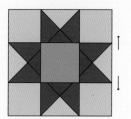

9. Sew 1 **triangle** to 2 opposite sides of **Star Unit** (**Fig. 7**). Sew 1 triangle to each remaining side of Star Unit to make **Block**. Making sure Star Unit is centered, trim Block to $11^7/8$" x $11^7/8$".

Fig. 7

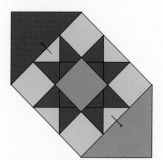

10. Repeat **Steps 1–9** to make 30 Blocks.

Block (make 30)

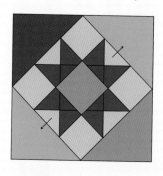

ASSEMBLING THE QUILT TOP CENTER

*Refer to **Quilt Top Diagram**, page 55, for placement.*
1. Sew 5 **Blocks** together to make **Row**. Press seam allowances open or in one direction in every other Row and in the opposite direction in remaining Rows. Row should measure $57^3/8$" x $11^7/8$". Make 6 **Rows**.
2. Sew **Rows** together, pressing seam allowances open or in one direction to make quilt top center. Quilt top center should measure $57^3/8$" x $68^3/4$".

ADDING THE INNER BORDER
1. Using diagonal seams (**Fig. 8**), sew **side border strips** together into a continuous strip. Press seam allowances open.

Fig. 8

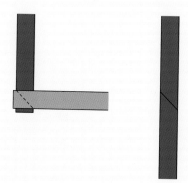

2. To determine length of **side inner borders**, measure *length* across center of quilt top center. Cut 2 side inner borders from continuous strip. Matching centers and corners, sew side inner borders to quilt top center. Press seam allowances to border.
3. Using diagonal seams, sew **top/bottom border strips** together into a continuous strip. Press seam allowances open.
4. To determine length of **top/bottom inner borders**, measure *width* across center of quilt top center (including added borders). Cut 2 top/bottom inner borders from continuous strip. Matching centers and corners, sew top/bottom inner borders to quilt top center. Press seam allowances to border.

ADDING THE OUTER BORDER
1. Draw a diagonal line (corner to corner) on wrong side of each light **large square**.
2. In the same manner as before, use 1 light **large square** and 1 dark **large square** to make 2 **Triangle-Square C's**. Triangle-Square C should measure $6^1/2$" x $6^1/2$". Make 48 Triangle-Square C's.

Triangle-Square C (make 48)

3. Sew 12 **Triangle-Square C's** together to make **side outer border**. Press seam allowances open or in one direction. Make 2 side outer borders.

Side Outer Border (make 2)

4. Measure *length* across center of quilt top. Measure length of side outer borders. If measurements are not the same, make seams in borders slightly larger or smaller as needed. Matching centers and corners, sew side outer borders to quilt top. Press seam allowances to inner border.

5. Sew 12 **Triangle-Square C's** together to make **top outer border**. Press seam allowances open or in one direction. Repeat to make **bottom outer border**.

Top/Bottom Outer Border (make 2)

6. Measure *width* across center of quilt top. Measure length of top/bottom outer borders. If measurements are not the same, make seams in borders slightly larger or smaller as needed. Matching centers and corners, sew top/bottom outer borders to quilt top. Quilt top should measure $72^3/8$" x $84^1/2$". Press seam allowances to inner border.

COMPLETING THE QUILT

1. To help stabilize the edges and prevent any seams from separating, stay-stitch around the quilt top approximately $1/8$" from the edge.

2. Follow **Machine Quilting**, page 107, to mark, layer, and quilt as desired. Quilt shown was machine quilted with an all-over design in the quilt center. The inner border is quilted with a loop pattern, and the outer border is quilted with fern patterns in the dark areas and a continuous pattern in the light areas.

3. Follow **Making a Hanging Sleeve**, page 109, if a hanging sleeve is desired.

4. Cut a 28" square of binding fabric. Follow **Binding**, page 109, to bind quilt using 2"w bias binding with mitered corners.

NOTE: This quilt can be made larger or smaller by adding or subtracting horizontal Rows or vertical Rows. Each Row will change the measurement of the quilt by $11^3/8$".

Due SOUTH

Quilted by Diane Tricka.

Finished Quilt Size:
72$\frac{1}{2}$" x 80$\frac{7}{8}$" (184 cm x 205 cm)

I love quilts with lots of triangles. It isn't a secret, is it? Almost every piece in this quilt is a triangle! How cool is that? Do you think my love affair with triangles and flying geese might mean that I liked geometry more than I thought I did? I've come to terms with my affection for math, but having to accept that I really did like geometry might be more than I could bear.

Suffice it to say, if you love making Flying Geese, this is the quilt for you. All you need is pretty fabric.

Geese are known for flying south for the winter. And *Due South* was the name of a really good television show about a Canadian Mountie who came south to Chicago. I thought the name fit, even though the geese seem to be flying northeast on my quilt. It just doesn't look right when you turn it the other way. And since I get to name it, I called it "Due South."

Yardage Requirements

Yardage is based on 43"/44" (109 cm/112 cm) wide fabric. Fat quarters are approximately 21" x 18" (53 cm x 46 cm).

> 21 fat quarters of assorted light print fabrics
> 14 fat quarters of assorted dark print fabrics
> $^7/_8$ yd (80 cm) of fabric for binding
> $6^3/_4$ yds (6.2 m)* of fabric for backing

You will also need:

> 81" x 89" (206 cm x 226 cm) piece of batting

> *Yardage is based on three 81" (206 cm) lengths of fabric, which allows for a larger backing for long arm quilting. If you are using another quilting method, two 89" (226 cm) lengths or 5 yds (4.6 m), will be adequate.

Cutting Out the Pieces

*Follow **Rotary Cutting**, page 105, to cut fabric. All measurements include $^1/_4$" seam allowances.*

From *each* of 8 assorted light print fat quarters:

- Cut 2 **border strips** $6^1/_2$" x 21". Cut a total of 16 border strips.
- Cut 1 strip $3^7/_8$" x 21". From this strip,
  - Cut 4 **medium squares** $3^7/_8$" x $3^7/_8$". Cut a total of 28 medium squares.

From *each* of 7 assorted light print fat quarters:

- Cut 1 strip 6" x 21". From this strip,
  - Cut 2 squares 6" x 6". Cut a total of 12 squares. Cut squares *once* diagonally to make 24 **triangles**.
  - Cut 1 **medium square** $3^7/_8$" x $3^7/_8$". Cut a total of 7 medium squares.
- Cut 3 strips $3^7/_8$" x 21". From these strips,
  - Cut 15 **medium squares** $3^7/_8$" x $3^7/_8$". Cut a total of 105 medium squares.

From *each* of 6 assorted light print fat quarters:

- Cut 2 strips $3^7/_8$" x 21". From these strips
  - Cut 10 **medium squares** $3^7/_8$" x $3^7/_8$". Cut a total of 60 medium squares.
- Cut 1 strip $4^1/_4$" x 21". From this strip,
  - Cut 2 **large squares** $4^1/_4$" x $4^1/_4$". Cut a total of 12 large squares.
  - Cut 2 **medium squares** $3^7/_8$" x $3^7/_8$". Cut a total of 12 medium squares. You will have 212 (53 sets of 4 matching) medium squares.
- Cut 1 strip 2" x 21". From this strip,
  - Cut 8 **very small squares** 2" x 2". Cut a total of 44 (11 sets of 4 matching) very small squares.

From *each* of 11 assorted dark print fabrics:

- Cut 2 strips $7^1/_4$" x 21". From these strips
  - Cut 4 **very large squares** $7^1/_4$" x $7^1/_4$". Cut a total of 44 very large squares.
  - Cut 1 **center square** $3^1/_2$" x $3^1/_2$". Cut a total of 11 center squares.
- Cut 1 strip $2^3/_8$" x 21". From this strip,
  - Cut 4 **small squares** $2^3/_8$" x $2^3/_8$". Cut a total of 44 (11 sets of 4 matching) small squares.

From *each* of 3 assorted dark print fabrics:

- Cut 2 strips $7^1/_4$" x 21". From these strips
  - Cut 3 **very large squares** $7^1/_4$" x $7^1/_4$". Cut a total of 9 very large squares. You will have 53 very large squares.

Making the Large Flying Geese

*Follow **Piecing**, page 106, and **Pressing**, page 107, to assemble quilt top. Because there are so many seams in this quilt, you may need to use a seam allowance slightly smaller than the usual $^1/_4$".*

As you sew, measure your work to compare with the measurements provided, which include seam allowances, and adjust your seam allowance as needed. Arrows on diagrams indicate suggested directions to press seam allowances.

1. For 4 **Large Flying Geese**, select 4 matching light **medium squares** and 1 dark **very large square**.
2. Draw a diagonal line (corner to corner) on wrong side of each **medium square**.

. Matching right sides, place 1 **medium square** on opposite corners of **very large square** (**Fig. 1**); pin in place.

Fig. 1

. Stitch ¹/₄" from each side of drawn lines (**Fig. 2**). Cut along drawn lines to make 2 **Unit 1's**.

Fig. 2   **Unit 1** (make 2)

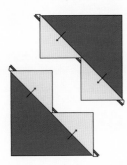

. Matching corners, place 1 **medium square** on each **Unit 1**. Stitch seam ¹/₄" from each side of drawn lines (**Fig. 3**). Cut along drawn lines to make 4 **Large Flying Geese**. Large Flying Geese should measure 6¹/₂" x 3¹/₂".

. Repeat **Steps 1–5** to make 212 (53 sets of 4 matching) Large Flying Geese.

Fig. 3   **Large Flying Geese**
(make 53 sets of 4 matching)

MAKING THE SMALL FLYING GEESE

1. For 4 matching **Small Flying Geese**, select 1 light print **large square** and 4 matching dark print **small squares**.
2. Draw a diagonal line (corner to corner) on wrong side of each **small square**.
3. In the same manner as before, make 4 matching **Small Flying Geese**. Small Flying Geese should measure 3¹/₂" x 2".
4. Repeat **Steps 1–3** to make 44 (11 sets of 4 matching) Small Flying Geese. You will have 1 large square left over.

Small Flying Geese
(make 11 sets of 4 matching)

MAKING THE STAR BLOCKS

1. For **Star Block**, select 4 matching **Small Flying Geese**, 4 **very small squares** (the same fabric as the light print in the Small Flying Geese), and 1 **center square** (the same fabric as the dark print in the Small Flying Geese).
2. Sew 2 **very small squares** and 1 **Small Flying Geese** together to make **Unit 2**. Make 2 Unit 2's.
3. Sew 2 **Small Flying Geese** and 1 **center square** together to make **Unit 3**.

Unit 2 (make 2)   **Unit 3**

          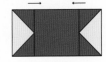

4. Sew 2 **Unit 2's** and **Unit 3** together to make **Star Block**. Star Block should measure 6¹/₂" x 6¹/₂".
5. Repeat **Steps 1–4** to make 11 Star Blocks.

Star Block (make 11)

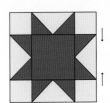

MAKING THE SETTING TRIANGLES

Some of the triangles for the side settings will be cut from the border strips. These triangles and those cut earlier will be different sizes. They are all cut larger than needed, and will be trimmed after assembling the quilt top center.

1. On **border strips,** remove selvages and square short edges as needed.
2. Place 1 border strip right side up on cutting mat. Aligning the 45° line on ruler with short edge of border strip and with ruler's edge at corner of border strip, cut **triangle** as shown (**Fig. 4**). Rotate border strip and cut triangle from opposite end.

Fig. 4

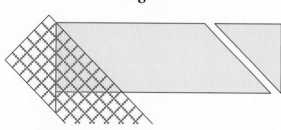

3. Repeat with remaining border strips to yield 32 **triangles**. You will have 56 triangles including those cut earlier.
4. Set aside 4 triangles of same size for the **corner setting triangles**.
5. Sew 2 triangles of same size together to make **side setting triangle**. Press seam allowances open or to one side. Make 26 side setting triangles.

Side Setting Triangle (make 26)

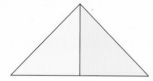

ASSEMBLING THE QUILT TOP CENTER

*Refer to **Assembly Diagram** for placement. The Star Blocks can be placed where desired.*

1. Select 38 **Large Flying Geese** with a variety of prints and colors for borders; set aside.

2. Sew remaining **Large Flying Geese, Star Blocks,** and **side setting triangles** into diagonal **Rows**. Press seam allowances open or press them in one direction in every other Row and in the opposite direction in remaining Rows.
3. Sew **Rows** and **corner setting triangles** together to complete quilt top center. Press seam allowances open or in one direction.
4. Trim quilt top center so that corner seams of Blocks and Flying Geese are $1/2$" from edge of quilt top center. Quilt top center should measure approximately $60^1/_2$" x $68^7/_8$".

ADDING THE BORDERS

1. Sew 2 **Large Flying Geese** together to make Corner Unit. Press seam allowances open or to one side. **Corner Unit** should measure $6^1/_2$" x $6^1/_2$". Make 2 Corner Units.

Corner Unit (make 2)

2. Sew 4 **border strips** together to make **Unit 4**. Press seam allowances open or in one direction. Square 1 end. Make 4 Unit 4's.

Unit 4 (make 4)

3. Sew 11 **Large Flying Geese** and 1 **Unit 4** together to make **left border**. Press seam allowances open or in one direction.
4. Sew 10 **Large Flying Geese** and 1 **Unit 4** together to make **right border**. Press seam allowances open or in one direction.

4. To determine length to trim **side borders**, measure *length* across center of quilt top center. Trim Unit 4 end of side borders to determined length. Matching centers and corners, sew side borders to quilt top center. Press seam allowances to borders.

5. Sew 1 **Corner Unit**, 6 **Large Flying Geese**, and 1 **Unit** 4 together to make **top border**. Press seam allowances open or in one direction.

6. Sew 1 **Corner Unit**, 7 **Large Flying Geese**, and 1 **Unit** 4 together to make **bottom border**. Press seam allowances open or in one direction.

7. To determine length to trim **top/bottom borders**, measure *width* across center of quilt top center (including added borders). Trim Unit 4 end of top/bottom borders to

determined length. Matching centers and corners, sew top/bottom borders to quilt top center. Press seam allowances to borders. Quilt top should measure approximately $72^1/_2$" x $80^7/_8$"

COMPLETING THE QUILT

1. To help stabilize the edges and prevent any seams from separating, stay-stitch around quilt top approximately $^1/_8$" from the edge.

2. Follow **Machine Quilting**, page 107, to mark, layer, and quilt as desired. Quilt shown was machine quilted.

3. Follow **Making a Hanging Sleeve**, page 109, if a hanging sleeve is desired.

4. Cut a 27" square of binding fabric. Follow **Binding**, page 109, to bind quilt using 2"w bias binding with mitered corners.

Assembly Diagram

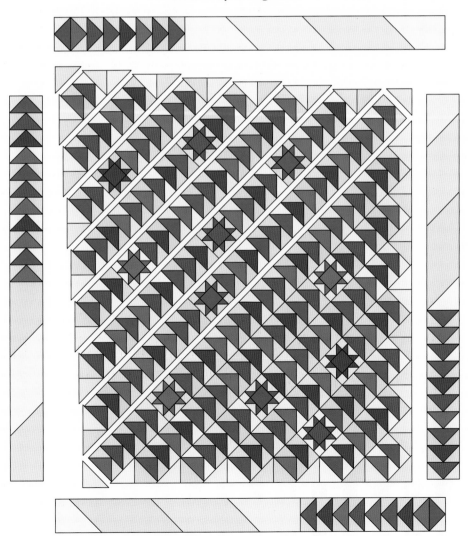

Allemande

Quilted by Louise Haley.

Finished Quilt Size:
78$^1/_4$" x 78$^1/_4$" (199 cm x 199 cm)
Finished Block Size:
12" x 12" (30 cm x 30 cm)

It started with an antique two-color quilt. Something about the design stuck in my head. I think it was the pinwheels. They just kept dancing around, calling my name. But I just wasn't in a two-color kind of mood. Then I saw this wonderful floral print that just needed to be used in big pieces. It had all kinds of colors that could be pulled out for accents, and I didn't want anything to compete with the floral print so the other fabrics had to be in small pieces—so what about pinwheels?

And since pinwheels look like they have a "dance" thing going on, all that swaying back and forth, I named this quilt "Allemande." It's a term used in square dancing. It actually means, "a step to the side." I also admit that I just like the way the word sounds. "Allemande."

YARDAGE REQUIREMENTS

Yardage is based on 43"/44" (109 cm/112 cm) wide fabric. Fat quarters are approximately 21" x 18" (53 cm x 46 cm).

- 9 fat quarters of assorted (light, medium, and dark) print fabrics
- $3^3/_4$ yds (3.4 m) of tan print fabric
- $2^3/_4$ yds (2.5 m) of yellow floral fabric
- 1 yd (91 cm) of fabric for binding
- $7^1/_4$ yds (6.6 m) of fabric for backing

You will also need:

- 86" x 86" (218 cm x 218 cm) piece of batting
- Template plastic
- Permanent marker
- Chalk pencil

CUTTING OUT THE PIECES

*Follow **Rotary Cutting**, page 105, to cut fabric. All measurements include $^1/_4$" seam allowances.*

From *each* assorted print fat quarter:
- Cut 4 strips $4^1/_4$" x 21". From these strips,
  - Cut 16 **medium squares** $4^1/_4$" x $4^1/_4$". Cut a total of 144 medium squares.

From tan print fabric:
- Cut 8 strips $6^7/_8$" x the width of the fabric. From these strips,
  - Cut 36 **large squares** $6^7/_8$" x $6^7/_8$".
- Cut 12 strips $4^1/_4$" x the width of the fabric. From these strips,
  - Cut 108 **medium squares** $4^1/_4$" x $4^1/_4$".
- Cut 4 strips $3^7/_8$" x the width of the fabric. From these strips,
  - Cut 36 **small squares** $3^7/_8$" x $3^7/_8$".

From yellow floral fabric:
- Cut 1 strip $6^7/_8$" x the width of the fabric. From this strip,
  - Cut 5 **large squares** $6^7/_8$" x $6^7/_8$".
- Cut 4 *lengthwise* **borders** $4^3/_4$" x 81".
- *From remaining width,*
  - Cut 11 strips $6^7/_8$" x 21". From these strips,
    - Cut 31 **large squares** $6^7/_8$" x $6^7/_8$". You will have 36 large squares.

MAKING THE TRIANGLE-SQUARES

*Follow **Piecing**, page 106, and **Pressing**, page 107, to assemble quilt top. Because there are so many seams in this quilt, you may need to use a seam allowance slightly smaller than the usual $^1/_4$". As you sew, measure your work to compare with the measurements provided, which include seam allowances, and adjust your seam allowance as needed. Arrows on diagrams indicate suggested directions to press seam allowances.*

1. Draw a diagonal line (corner to corner) on wrong side of each tan **large square**.
2. Matching right sides, place 1 tan **large square** on top of 1 yellow **large square**. Stitch $^1/_4$" from each side of drawn line (**Fig. 1**). Cut along drawn line and press seam allowances to yellow fabric to make 2 **Triangle-Square A's**. Triangle-Square A should measure $6^1/_2$" x $6^1/_2$". Make 72 Triangle-Square A's.

Fig. 1

Triangle-Square A (make 72)

3. Draw a diagonal line (corner to corner) on wrong side of each tan **medium square**.

In the same manner as before, use tan **medium squares** and assorted print **medium squares** to make 216 **Triangle-Square B's**. Triangle-Square B should measure $3^7/_8$" x $3^7/_8$".

Triangle-Square B (make 216)

. Draw a diagonal line (corner to corner) on wrong side of 18 assorted print **medium squares**.

. In the same manner as before, use marked assorted print **medium squares** and unmarked assorted print **medium squares** to make 36 **Triangle-Square C's**. Triangle-Square C should measure $3^7/_8$" x $3^7/_8$".

Triangle-Square C (make 36)

MAKING THE PIECED UNITS

. Draw a diagonal line (corner to corner and perpendicular to seam) on wrong side of 72 **Triangle-Square B's**.

. Matching right sides and seams and with like fabrics opposite, place 1 marked **Triangle-Square B** on top of 1 unmarked **Triangle-Square B**. Stitch $^1/_4$" from each side of drawn line (**Fig. 2**). Cut along drawn line and press seam allowances to one side to make 2 **Unit 1's**. Unit 1 should measure $3^1/_2$" x $3^1/_2$". Make 144 Unit 1's.

Fig. 2

Unit 1 (make 144)

3. Draw a diagonal line (corner to corner and perpendicular to seam) on wrong side of 36 **Triangle-Square B's**.

4. Matching right sides and seams, place 1 marked **Triangle-Square B** on top of 1 **Triangle-Square C**. In the same manner as before, make 2 **Unit 2's**. Unit 2 should measure $3^1/_2$" x $3^1/_2$". Make 72 Unit 2's.

Unit 2 (make 72)

5. Draw a diagonal line (corner to corner) on wrong side of each tan **small square**.

6. Matching right sides, place 1 tan small square on top of 1 **Triangle-Square B**. Stitch $^1/_4$" from each side of drawn line (**Fig. 3**). Cut along drawn line and press seam allowances to larger triangle to make 2 **Unit 3's**. Unit 3 should measure $3^1/_2$" x $3^1/_2$". (*Note: Units will be mirror images of each other, but this will not effect the appearance of the quilt.*) Make 72 Unit 3's.

Fig. 3

Unit 3 (make 72)

 or

7. Sew 1 **Unit 1** and 1 **Unit 2** together to make **Unit 4**. Make 72 Unit 4's.

Unit 4 (make 72)

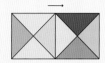

8. Sew 1 **Unit 1** and 1 **Unit 3** together to make **Unit 5**. Make 72 Unit 5's.

Unit 5 (make 72)

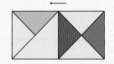 *or*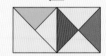

9. Sew 1 **Unit 4** and 1 **Unit 5** together to make **Pieced Unit**. To press seam allowances, follow **Collapsing the Seams**, page 107. Pieced Unit should measure $6^1/2$" x $6^1/2$". Make 72 Pieced Units.

Pieced Unit (make 72)

MAKING THE BLOCKS

1. Sew 2 **Pieced Units** together to make **Unit 6**. Unit 6 should measure $12^1/2$" x $6^1/2$". Make 34 Unit 6's.

Unit 6 (make 34)

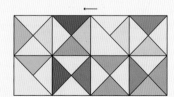

2. Sew 2 **Unit 6's** together to make **Pieced Block**. In the same manner as before, press seam allowances by "collapsing the seams." Pieced Block should measure $12^1/2$" x $12^1/2$". Make 13 Pieced Blocks.

Pieced Block (make 13)

3. Sew 2 **Triangle-Square A's** together to make **Unit 7**. Unit 7 should measure $12^1/2$" x $6^1/2$". Make 36 Unit 7's.

Unit 7 (make 36)

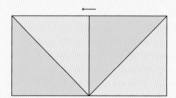

4. Sew 2 **Unit 7's** together to make **Pinwheel Block**. In the same manner as before, press seam allowances by "collapsing the seams." Pinwheel Block should measure $12^1/2$" x $12^1/2$". Make 12 Pinwheel Blocks.

Pinwheel Block (make 12)

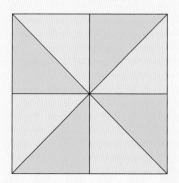

ASSEMBLING THE QUILT TOP CENTER

Refer to Assembly Diagram, page 68, for placement.

1. Sew 2 **Pieced Units**, 2 **Unit 6's**, and 3 **Unit 7's** together to make **Row A**. Press seam allowances open or in one direction. Row A should measure $72^1/2$" x $6^1/2$". Make 2 Row A's.

2. Sew 2 **Unit 7's**, 3 **Pieced Blocks**, and 2 **Pinwheel Blocks** together to make **Row B**. Press seam allowances open or in the opposite direction of Row A's. Row B should measure $72^1/2$" x $12^1/2$". Make 3 Row B's.

3. Sew 2 **Unit 6's**, 3 **Pinwheel Blocks**, and 2 **Pieced Blocks** together to make **Row C**. Press seam allowances open or in the same direction as Row A's. Row C should measure $72^1/2$" x $12^1/2$". Make 2 Row C's.

4. Sew **Rows** together to make quilt top center. Press seam allowances open or in one direction. Quilt top center should measure $72^1/2$" x $72^1/2$".

ADDING THE BORDER

1. Mark the center of each edge of quilt top center. Mark the center of 1 long edge of each **border**.

2. Measure across center of quilt top. Matching center marks and raw edges, pin 1 border to center of quilt top edge. From center of border, measure out $1/2$ the width of the quilt top in both directions and mark. Match marks on border with corners of quilt top and pin. Easing in any fullness, pin border to quilt top between center and corners. Sew border to quilt top, beginning and ending exactly $1/4$" from each corner of quilt top and backstitching at beginning and ending of stitching.

3. Repeat **Step 2** to sew border to bottom edge of quilt top. Fold and pin ends of top and bottom borders out of the way, and then sew remaining borders to side edges of quilt top.

4. Fold 1 corner of quilt top diagonally with right sides together and matching edges. Aligning ruler with fold, use ruler to mark stitching line as shown in **Fig. 4**. Sew on drawn line, backstitching at beginning and ending of stitching.

Fig. 4

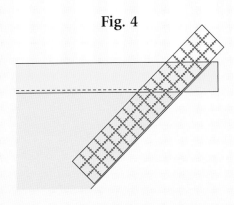

5. Turn mitered corner right side up. Check to make sure corner will lie flat with no gaps or puckers. Trim seam allowances to $1/4$" and press to one side. Repeat for remaining corners. Press seam allowances to border.

6. To make templates for scalloped edge, use permanent marker and trace **scallop patterns**, page 69, onto template plastic. Cut templates out along traced lines.

7. Using templates and chalk pencil, lightly trace around templates to mark scallops in borders. Once scallops are marked as desired, trace over drawn lines with a more durable marker, such as a lead pencil. *Do not cut scallops at this time.*

COMPLETING THE QUILT

1. Follow **Machine Quilting**, page 107, to mark, layer, and quilt as desired. Quilt shown was machine quilted with a meandering loop pattern in the tan areas. Curved triangles were quilted in each assorted fabric triangle. A flower with leaves was quilted in each yellow floral triangle and a feather pattern was quilted $3/8$" from the scalloped edge of the border.

2. Cut a 29" square of binding fabric. Follow **Binding**, page 109, to bind quilt using 2"w bias binding on scalloped-edge quilts.

NOTE: This quilt can be made larger or smaller by adding or subtracting horizontal Rows or vertical Rows. Each Row will change the measurement of the quilt by 12".

Assembly Diagram

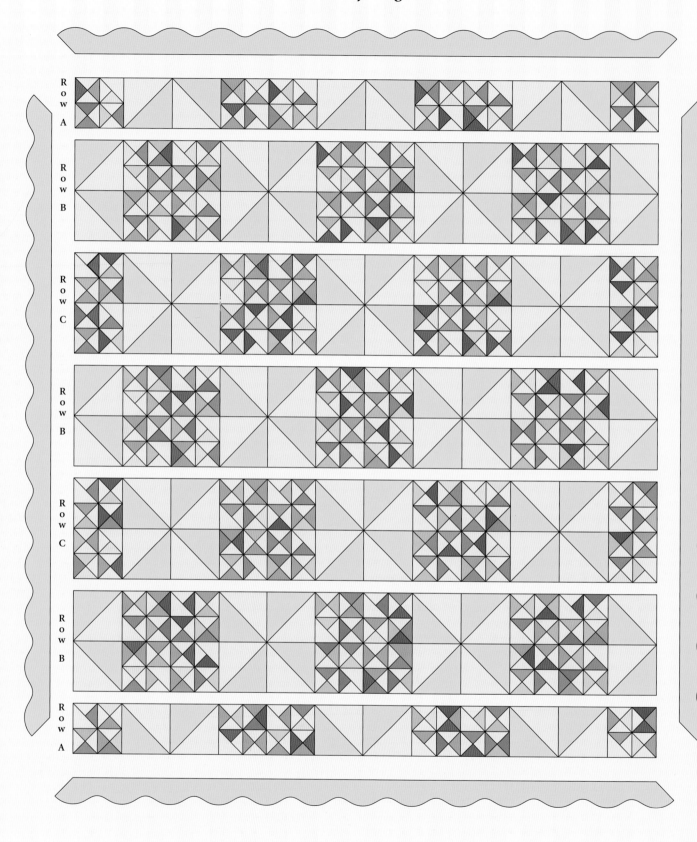

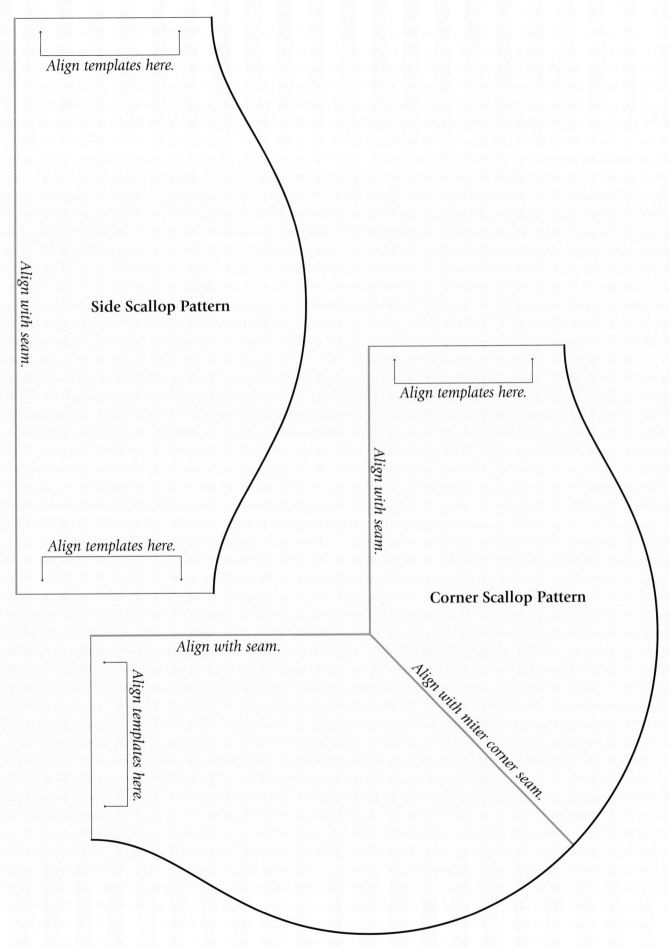

Align templates here.

Align with seam.

Side Scallop Pattern

Align templates here.

Align templates here.

Align with seam.

Corner Scallop Pattern

Align with seam.

Align templates here.

Align with miter corner seam.

69

Simple CITY

Quilted by Louise Haley.

Finished Quilt Size:
81¹/₂" x 81¹/₂" (207 cm x 207 cm)
Finished Block Size:
9" x 9" (23 cm x 23 cm)

May it please the court…I have been charged with false advertising because I named a quilt with 926 pieces "Simple City." I intend to argue that a quilt with a lot of pieces is not necessarily a difficult quilt, just as the time spent making a quilt is not the same thing as the level of skill required.

As you may know, I love quilts that look like something you might throw on the hammock on a summer day. Well, not a summer day in Phoenix—who has a hammock in their house? Anyway, the soft, summertime colors and beautiful prints in these fabrics would have been lost if I had cut them into little-bitty pieces.

The name of this quilt came from my friend Tuesday Sue. I told her I wanted a simple name, something that fit what was essentially a pretty simple quilt. She laughed and said that her boys always called the things they deemed easy, "simple city." And there you have it.

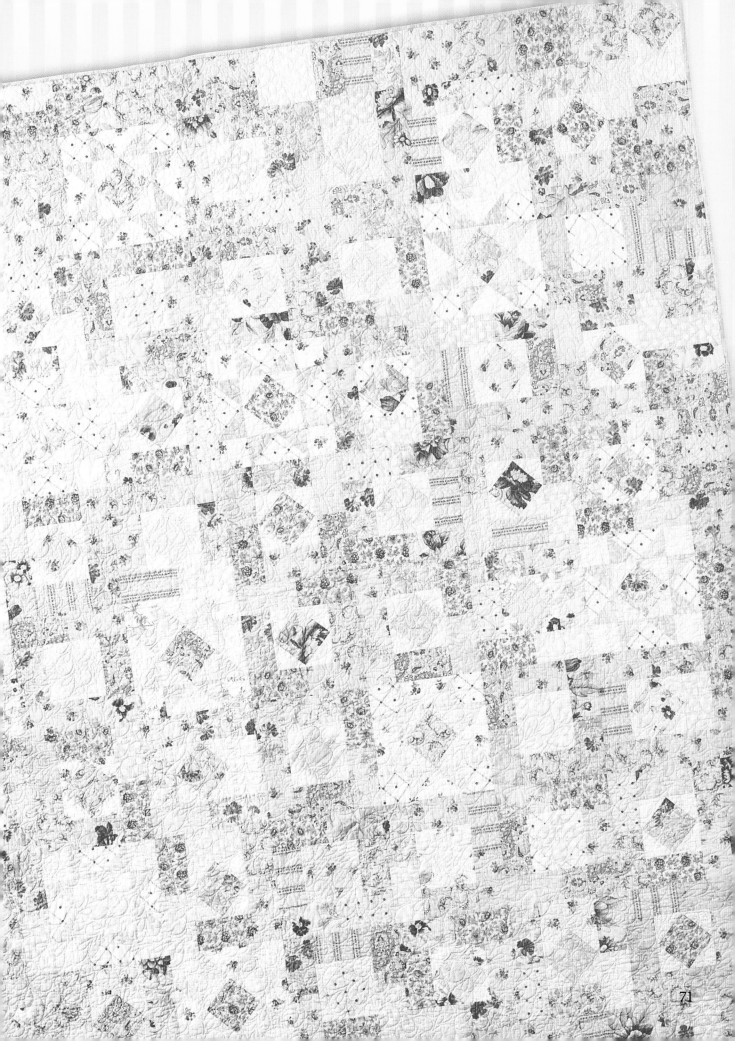

Yardage Requirements

Yardage is based on 43"/44" (109 cm/112 cm) wide fabric. Fat quarters are approximately 21" x 18" (53 cm x 46 cm).

> 10 fat quarters of assorted light print fabrics
> 25 fat quarters of assorted pastel (pink, yellow, blue, and green) print fabrics
> $^7/_8$ yd (80 cm) of fabric for binding
> $7^1/_2$ yds (6.9 m) of fabric for backing

You will also need:

> 90" x 90" (229 cm x 229 cm) piece of batting

Cutting Out the Pieces

*Follow **Rotary Cutting**, page 105, to cut fabric. All measurements include $^1/_4$" seam allowances. Triangles are larger than needed and will be trimmed.*

From *each* of 6 assorted light print fat quarters:

- Cut 1 strip $5^3/_4$" x 21". From this strip,
  - Cut 2 **very large squares** $5^3/_4$" x $5^3/_4$". Cut a total of 12 very large squares.
  - Cut 1 **small square** $2^3/_4$" x $2^3/_4$". Cut a total of 6 small squares.
- Cut 1 strip $2^3/_4$" x 21". From this strip,
  - Cut 7 **small squares** $2^3/_4$" x $2^3/_4$". Cut a total of 42 small squares. You will have 48 (12 sets of 4 matching) small squares.
- Cut 2 strips $3^3/_8$" x 21". From these strips,
  - Cut 12 squares $3^3/_8$" x $3^3/_8$". Cut a total of 72 squares. Cut each square *once* diagonally to make 144 **triangles**.

From *each* of 4 remaining assorted light print fat quarters:

- Cut 3 strips $3^3/_8$" x 21". From these strips,
  - Cut 16 squares $3^3/_8$" x $3^3/_8$". Cut a total of 64 squares. Cut each square *once* diagonally to make 128 **triangles**. You will have 272 (68 sets of 4 matching) triangles.

From *each* of 12 assorted pastel print fat quarters:

- Cut 1 strip $3^5/_8$" x 21". From this strip,
  - Cut 2 **center squares** $3^5/_8$" x $3^5/_8$". Cut a total of 24 center squares.
  - Cut 4 **medium squares** $3^1/_8$" x $3^1/_8$". Cut a total of 48 (12 sets of 4 matching) medium squares.
- Cut 1 strip 5" x 21". From this strip,
  - Cut 1 **large square** 5" x 5". Cut a total of 12 large squares.
  - Cut 5 **rectangles** $2^3/_4$" x 5". Cut a total of 60 rectangles.
- Cut 3 strips $2^3/_4$" x 21". From these strips,
  - Cut 12 **rectangles** $2^3/_4$" x 5". Cut a total of 144 rectangles.

From *each* of 13 remaining assorted pastel print fat quarters:

- Cut 1 strip $3^5/_8$" x 21". From this strip,
  - Cut 4 **center squares** $3^5/_8$" x $3^5/_8$". Cut a total of 44 center squares. You will have 68 center squares.
- Cut 1 strip 5" x 21". Cut a total of 13 strips.
  - From 1 of these strips,
    - Cut 2 **large squares** 5" x 5".
  - From *each* of 12 of these strips,
    - Cut 1 **large square** 5" x 5". Cut a total of 12 large squares. You will have 26 large squares.
    - Cut 3 **rectangles** 5" x $2^3/_4$". Cut a total of 36 rectangles.
- Cut 3 strips $2^3/_4$" x 21". From these strips,
  - Cut 12 **rectangles** $2^3/_4$" x 5". Cut a total of 148 rectangles. You will have 388 rectangles.

MAKING THE ECONOMY PATCHES

Follow **Piecing**, page 106, and **Pressing**, page 107, to assemble quilt top. Because there are so many seams in this quilt, you may need to use a seam allowance slightly smaller than the usual ¹/₄". As you sew, measure your work to compare with the measurements provided, which include seam allowances, and adjust your seam allowance as needed. Arrows on diagrams indicate suggested directions to press seam allowances.

1. For **Economy Patch**, select 4 matching light **triangles** and 1 pastel **center square**.
2. Sew 1 **triangle** to 2 opposite sides of **center square** (**Fig. 1**). Sew remaining **triangles** to center square to make **Economy Patch**. Making sure center square is centered, trim Economy Patch to 5" x 5".
3. Repeat **Steps 1–2** to make 68 Economy Patches.

Fig. 1

Economy Patch (make 68)

MAKING THE FLYING GEESE

1. For 4 matching **Flying Geese**, select 4 matching pastel **medium squares** and 1 light **very large square**.
2. Draw a diagonal line (corner to corner) on wrong side of each pastel **medium square**.
3. Matching right sides, place 1 **medium square** on opposite corners of **very large square** (**Fig. 2**); pin in place.

Fig. 2

4. Stitch ¹/₄" from each side of drawn lines (**Fig. 3**). Cut along drawn lines to make 2 **Unit 1's**.

Fig. 3   **Unit 1** (make 2)

5. Matching corners, place 1 **medium square** on each **Unit 1**. Stitch seam ¹/₄" from each side of drawn lines (**Fig. 4**). Cut along drawn lines to make 4 **Flying Geese**. Flying Geese should measure 5" x 2³/₄".

Fig. 4

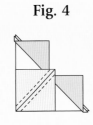

6. Repeat **Steps 1–5** to make 12 sets of 4 matching Flying Geese.

Flying Geese (make 12 sets of 4 matching)

MAKING THE BLOCK A'S

1. For **Block A**, select 6 **rectangles** of the same color (but assorted prints) and 1 **Economy Patch**.
2. Sew 2 **rectangles** together to make **Unit 2**. Make 2 Unit 2's.
3. Sew 2 **rectangles** and **Economy Patch** together to make **Unit 3**.

Unit 2   Unit 3
(make 2)

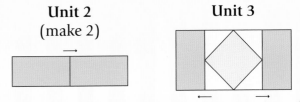

73

4. Sew 2 **Unit 2's** and **Unit 3** together to make **Block A**. Block A should measure 9¹/₂" x 9¹/₂".

5. Repeat **Steps 1–4** to make 52 Block A's.

Block A (make 52)

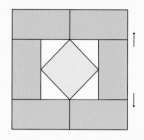

MAKING THE BLOCK B'S

1. For **Block B**, select 1 **Economy Patch**, 4 matching **Flying Geese**, and 4 matching light **small squares**.

2. Sew 1 **Flying Geese** and 2 **small squares** together to make **Unit 4**. Make 2 Unit 4's.

3. Sew 2 **Flying Geese** and **Economy Patch** together to make **Unit 5**.

Unit 4 (make 2)   **Unit 5**

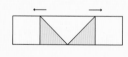   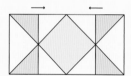

4. Sew 2 **Unit 4's** and **Unit 5** together to make **Block B**. Block B should measure 9¹/₂" x 9¹/₂".

5. Repeat **Steps 1–4** to make 12 Block B's.

Block B (make 12)

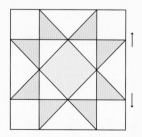

ASSEMBLING THE QUILT TOP CENTER

*Refer to **Quilt Top Diagram** for placement.*

1. Rotating every other Block, sew 8 **Blocks** together to make **Row**. Press seam allowances open or press them in one direction in every other Row and in the opposite direction in remaining Rows. Row should measure 72¹/₂" x 9¹/₂". Make 8 Rows.

2. Sew **Rows** together to make quilt top center. Press seam allowances open or in one direction. Quilt top center should measure 72¹/₂" x 72¹/₂".

ADDING THE BORDER

1. In desired order, sew 6 pastel **large squares** and 20 pastel **rectangles** together to make **side border**. Press seam allowances open or in one direction. Make 2 side borders.

2. Measure *length* across center of quilt top center. Measure length of side borders. If measurements are not the same, make seams in borders slightly larger or smaller as needed. Matching centers and corners, sew side borders to quilt top center. Press seam allowances to borders.

3. In desired order, sew 7 pastel **large squares** and 18 pastel **rectangles** together. Sew 1 **Economy Patch** to each end to make **top border**. Press seam allowances open or in one direction. Repeat to make **bottom border**.

4. Measure *width* across center of quilt top center (including added borders). Measure length of top/bottom borders. If measurements are not the same, make seams in borders slightly larger or smaller as needed. Matching centers and corners, sew top/bottom borders to quilt top center. Press seam allowances to borders. Quilt top should measure 81¹/₂" x 81¹/₂".

COMPLETING THE QUILT

1. To help stabilize the edges and prevent any seams from separating, stay-stitch around quilt top approximately $1/8$" from the edge.

2. Follow **Machine Quilting**, page 107, to mark, layer, and quilt as desired. Quilt shown was machine quilted with an all over swirling pattern.

3. Follow **Making a Hanging Sleeve**, page 109, if a hanging sleeve is desired.

4. Cut a 28" square of binding fabric. Follow **Binding**, page 109, to bind quilt using 2"w bias binding with mitered corners.

NOTE: This quilt can be made larger or smaller by adding or subtracting horizontal Rows or vertical Rows. Each Row will change the measurement of the quilt by 9".

Quilt Top Diagram

Quadrille

Quilted by Louise Haley.

Finished Quilt Size:
85" x 85" (216 cm x 216 cm)
Finished Block Size:
12³/₄" x 12³/₄" (32 cm x 32 cm)

As much as I liked this fabric when I saw it, I didn't have a clue what I was going to make with it. After much sketching and tearing up of paper—that's how I work out quilt ideas—I was getting a little desperate. I wanted big pieces to show off the pretty flowers, but I also really liked the dark pink and wanted those to be small pieces. That's when inspiration struck. I wish I could tell you this was a 100% original idea, but this nine-patch variation has been around as long as there have been quilters. But I'm sure everyone who preceded me didn't have such pretty fabric.

The dictionary says that a quadrille is "a square dance for four couples, consisting of five parts or movements, each complete in itself." So, work with me on this one: The quilt is square with four sides. The center nine-patch of each block has five pieced blocks—four corner blocks and one nine-patch. And it's complete.

Yardage Requirements

Yardage is based on 43"/44" (109 cm/112 cm) wide fabric. Fat quarters are approximately 21" x 18" (53 cm x 46 cm).

24 fat quarters of assorted pastel print and cream print fabrics

2 yds (1.8 m) of cream print fabric for Small Nine Patches

1^1/$_8$ yds (1 m) of rose print fabric

1 yd (91 cm) of fabric for binding

7^3/$_4$ yds (7.1 m) of fabric for backing

You will also need:

93" x 93" (236 cm x 236 cm) piece of batting

Cutting Out the Pieces

*Follow **Rotary Cutting**, page 105, to cut fabric. All measurements include ^{1}/$_4$" seam allowances. Triangles are slightly larger than needed and will be trimmed.*

From *each* pastel print fat quarter:

- Cut 1 strip 7^1/$_2$" x 21". From this strip,
  - Cut 2 squares 7^1/$_2$" x 7^1/$_2$". Cut a total of 48 squares. Cut squares *once* diagonally to make 96 **triangles**.
  - Cut 2 **squares** 3^1/$_2$" x 3^1/$_2$". Cut a total of 48 squares.
- Cut 1 strip 7^1/$_2$" x 21". From this strip,
  - Cut 1 square 7^1/$_2$" x 7^1/$_2$". Cut a total of 24 squares. Cut squares *once* diagonally to make 48 **triangles**. You will have 144 triangles.

    From remainder of strip,
    - Cut 2 strips 3^1/$_2$" x 13^1/$_2$". From *each* strip, cut
      - Cut 2 **squares** 3^1/$_2$" x 3^1/$_2$". Cut a total of 96 squares. You will have 144 squares.
      - Cut 1 **rectangle** 3^1/$_2$" x 6^1/$_2$". Cut a total of 44 rectangles.
- Cut 1 strip 2" x 21". From this strip,
  - Cut 2 **short strips** 7^1/$_2$" x 2". Cut a total of 25 short strips.

From cream print fabric for Small Nine Patches:

- Cut 11 strips 2^1/$_2$" x the width of the fabric. Cut these strips in half to make 22 **wide strips**. (You will use 21 and have 1 left over.)
- Cut 16 strips 1^1/$_2$" x the width of the fabric. Cut these strips in half to make 32 **narrow strips**.
- Cut 9 **inner border strips** 1^1/$_2$" x the width of the fabric.

From rose print fabric:

- Cut 23 strips 1^1/$_2$" x the width of the fabric. Cut these strips in half to make 46 **narrow strips**.

Making the Cream and Rose Units

*Follow **Piecing**, page 106, and **Pressing**, page 107, to assemble quilt top. Because there are so many seams in this quilt, you may need to use a seam allowance slightly smaller than the usual ^{1}/$_4$". As you sew, measure your work to compare with the measurements provided, which include seam allowances, and adjust your seam allowance as needed. Arrows on diagrams indicate suggested directions to press seam allowances.*

1. Sew 2 rose **narrow strips** and 1 cream **narrow strip** together to make **Strip Set A**. Strip Set A should measure 21" x 3^1/$_2$". Make 6 Strip Set A's. Cut across Strip Set A's at 1^1/$_2$" intervals to make 72 **Unit 1's**.

Strip Set A
(make 6)

Unit 1
(make 72)

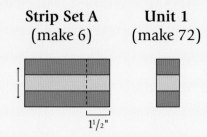

1^1/$_2$"

- Sew 2 cream **narrow strips** and 1 rose **narrow strip** together to make **Strip Set B**. Strip Set B should measure 21" x 3¹/₂". Make 13 Strip Set B's. Cut across Strip Set B's at 1¹/₂" intervals to make 180 **Unit 2's**.

Strip Set B (make 13)   **Unit 2** (make 180)

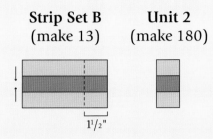

1¹/₂"

- Sew 1 rose **narrow strip** and 1 cream **wide strip** together to make **Strip Set C**. Strip Set C should measure 21" x 3¹/₂". Make 21 Strip Set C's. Cut across Strip Set C's at 1¹/₂" intervals to make 288 **Unit 3's**.

Strip Set C (make 21)   **Unit 3** (make 288)

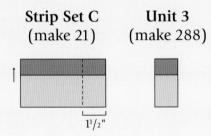

1¹/₂"

- Sew 2 **Unit 1's** and 1 **Unit 2** together to make **Small Nine Patch**. Small Nine Patch should measure 3¹/₂" x 3¹/₂". Make 36 Small Nine Patches.

Small Nine Patch (make 36)

- Sew 2 **Unit 3's** and 1 **Unit 2** together to make **Unit 4**. Unit 4 should measure 3¹/₂" x 3¹/₂". Make 144 Unit 4's.

Unit 4 (make 144)

MAKING THE BLOCKS

1. For **Block**, select 4 sets of 1 **triangle** and 1 **square** (each set from 1 fabric), 4 **Unit 4's**, and 1 **Small Nine Patch**.
2. Sew 2 **Unit 4's** and 1 **square** together to make **Unit 5**. Make 2 Unit 5's.
3. Sew 2 **squares** and 1 **Small Nine Patch** together to make **Unit 6**.

Unit 5 (make 2)   **Unit 6**

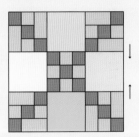

4. Sew 2 **Unit 5's** and **Unit 6** together to make **Large Nine Patch**. Large Nine Patch should measure 9¹/₂" x 9¹/₂".

Large Nine Patch

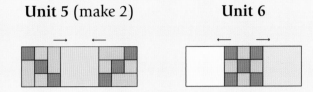

5. Sew 1 **triangle** to 2 opposite sides of **Large Nine Patch (Fig. 1)**. Sew 1 triangle to each remaining side of Large Nine Patch to make **Block**. Making sure Large Nine Patch is centered, trim Block to 13¹/₄" x 13¹/₄".
6. Repeat **Steps 1–5** to make a total of 36 Blocks.

Fig. 1   **Block** (make 36)

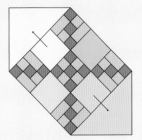
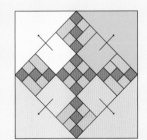

ASSEMBLING THE QUILT TOP CENTER
Refer to Quilt Top Diagram for placement.

1. Sew 6 **Blocks** together to make **Row**. Press seam allowances open or in one direction in every other Row and in the opposite direction in remaining Rows. Row should measure 77" x 13$^1/_4$". Make 6 Rows.
2. Sew **Rows** together to make quilt top center. Press seam allowances open or in one direction. Quilt top center should measure 77" x 77".

ADDING THE INNER BORDER

1. Using diagonal seams (**Fig. 2**), sew **inner border strips** together into a continuous strip. Press seam allowances open.

Fig. 2

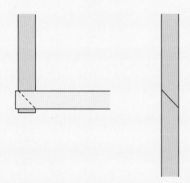

2. To determine length of **side inner borders**, measure *length* across center of quilt top center. Cut 2 side inner borders from continuous strip. Matching centers and corners, sew side inner borders to quilt top center. Press seam allowances to inner borders.
3. To determine length of **top/bottom inner borders**, measure *width* across center of quilt top center (including added borders). Cut 2 top/bottom inner borders from continuous strip. Matching centers and corners, sew top/bottom inner borders to quilt top center. Press seam allowances to inner borders.

ADDING THE OUTER BORDER

1. Sew 5 **short strips** together to make **Strip Set D**. Press seam allowances in one direction. Strip Set D should measure 7$^1/_2$" x 8". Make 5 Strip Sets D's. Cut across Strip Set D's at 3$^1/_2$" intervals to make 10 **Unit 7's**. Unit 7 should measure 3$^1/_2$" x 8".

Strip Set D (make 5)   **Unit 7** (make 10)

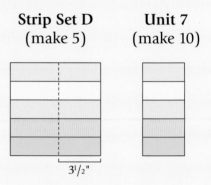

3$^1/_2$"

2. Sew 11 **rectangles** and 2 **Unit 7's** together to make **left outer border**. Press seam allowances open or in one direction.
3. Sew 10 **rectangles** and 3 **Unit 7's** together to make **right outer border**. Press seam allowances open or in one direction.
4. To determine length to trim **side outer borders**, measure *length* across center of quilt top. Trim borders to determined length. Matching centers and corners, sew side outer borders to quilt top. Press seam allowances to outer borders.
5. Sew 12 **rectangles** and 2 **Unit 7's** together to make **top outer border**. Press seam allowances open or in one direction.
6. Sew 11 **rectangles** and 3 **Unit 7's** together to make **bottom outer border**. Press seam allowances open or in one direction.
7. To determine length to trim **top/bottom outer borders**, measure *width* across center of quilt top (including added borders). Trim borders to determined length. Matching centers and corners, sew top/bottom outer borders to quilt top. Press seam allowances to outer borders. Quilt top should measure 85" x 85".

COMPLETING THE QUILT

. To help stabilize the edges and prevent any seams from separating, stay-stitch around quilt top approximately $^1/_8$" from the edge.

. Follow **Machine Quilting**, page 107, to mark, layer, and quilt as desired. Quilt shown was machine quilted. A feather pattern was quilted in the triangles. The cream areas of the Small Nine Patches were stipple quilted. Curvy lines were quilted in the squares and outer border. A loop pattern was quilted in the inner border.

3. Follow **Making a Hanging Sleeve**, page 109, if a hanging sleeve is desired.

4. Cut a 29" square of binding fabric. Follow **Binding**, page 109, to bind quilt using 2"w bias binding with mitered corners.

NOTE: This quilt can be made larger or smaller by adding or subtracting horizontal Rows or vertical Rows. Each Row will change the measurement of the quilt by $12^3/_4$". To make quilt slightly larger, add another plain or scrappy border.

Quilt Top Diagram

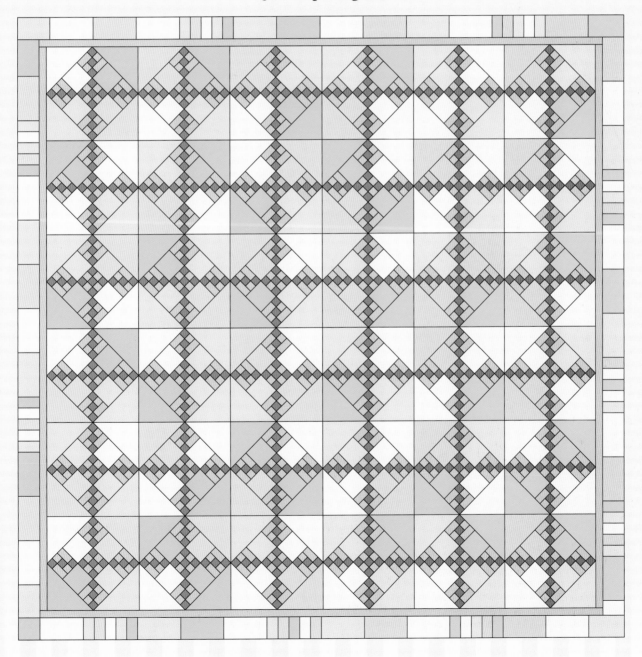

Sweet ESCAPE

Quilted by Louise Haley.

Finished Quilt Size:
69^1/$_2$" x 69^1/$_2$" (177 cm x 177 cm)
Finished Block Size:
7" x 7" (18 cm x 18 cm)

You may know from some of my other quilting escapades that I love puzzles, particularly the "how can I make this work" kind. I had a couple of layer cakes—precut 10" squares—that I really liked but didn't know what to make using them. Then I had a light-bulb moment. I made this quilt in two days! Of course, I sew fast and didn't have to read instructions to figure out what I was trying to do.

The Jewel Box blocks finish at 7" x 7". Each is made with two fabrics. You just cut out the pieces and mix-and-match the parts as you go along.

Naming this quilt was simple. Late one evening as I was finishing up the quilt, one of my favorite "drop-what-you're-doing-and-get-up-and-dance" songs started playing on my MP3 player. It occurred to me that since stitching and making quilts is always a "sweet escape," as is dancing around the room with Rosie, this was a perfect name for my quilt. Special thanks to Gwen Stefani for the terrific song, a little exercise, and a name for my quilt!

Yardage Requirements

Yardage is based on 43"/44" (109 cm/112 cm) wide fabric. Fat quarters are approximately 21" x 18" (53 cm x 46 cm). Layer cakes are approximately 10" x 10" (25 cm x 25 cm).

- 2 layer cakes (a total of 82 squares) *or* 24 fat quarters of assorted light, medium, and dark print fabrics
- $3/4$ yd (69 cm) of cream print fabric for setting triangles
- $7/8$ yd (80 cm) of fabric for binding
- $4^3/8$ yds (4 m) of fabric for backing

You will also need:

- 78" x 78" (198 cm x 198 cm) piece of batting

Cutting Out the Pieces

*Follow **Rotary Cutting**, page 105, to cut fabric. All measurements include $1/4$" seam allowances. Side and corner setting triangles are slightly larger than needed and will be trimmed.*

If using layer cakes—

From *each* of 61 layer cake squares (for Blocks):

- Cut 1 strip $4^3/8$" x 10". From this strip,
  - Cut 2 **squares** $4^3/8$" x $4^3/8$". Cut a total of 122 squares.
- Cut 2 **block strips** $2^1/4$" x 10". Cut a total of 122 strips.

From *each* of 6 layer cake squares (for border):

- Cut 2 **wide border strips** $2^3/4$" x 10". Cut a total of 8 wide border strips.
- Cut 2 **narrow border strips** $2^1/4$" x 10". Cut a total of 8 narrow border strips.

From *each* of 15 layer cake squares (for border):

- Cut 4 **narrow border strips** $2^1/4$" x 10". Cut a total of 60 narrow border strips. You will have 68 narrow border strips.

If using fat quarters—

From *each* of 8 fat quarters:

- Cut 1 strip $4^3/8$" x 21". From this strip,
  - Cut 4 **squares** $4^3/8$" x $4^3/8$". Cut a total of 32 squares.
- Cut 1 strip 5" x 21". From this strip,
  - Cut 1 rectangle 5" x 10". From this rectangle,
    - Cut 1 **wide border strip** $2^3/4$" x 10". Cut a total of 8 wide border strips.
    - Cut 1 **block strip** $2^1/4$" x 10". Cut a total of 8 block strips.
  - Cut 1 **square** $4^3/8$" x $4^3/8$". Cut a total of 8 squares.
- Cut 3 strips $2^1/4$" x 21". From these strips,
  - Cut 4 **block strips** $2^1/4$" x 10". Cut a total of 32 block strips.
  - Cut 2 **narrow border strips** $2^1/4$" x 10". Cut a total of 16 narrow border strips.

From *each* of 12 fat quarters:

- Cut 1 strip $4^3/8$" x 21". From this strip,
  - Cut 4 **squares** $4^3/8$" x $4^3/8$". Cut a total of 48 squares.
- Cut 1 strip $4^1/2$" x 21". From this strip,
  - Cut 1 rectangle $4^1/2$" x 10". From this rectangle,
    - Cut 2 **block strips** $2^1/4$" x 10". Cut a total of 24 block strips.
  - Cut 1 **square** $4^3/8$" x $4^3/8$". Cut a total of 12 squares.
- Cut 3 strips $2^1/4$" x 21". From these strips,
  - Cut 3 **block strips** $2^1/4$" x 10". Cut a total of 36 block strips.
  - Cut 3 **narrow border strips** $2^1/4$" x 10". Cut a total of 36 narrow border strips.

From *each* of 4 fat quarters:
- Cut 1 strip $4^3/8$" x 21". From this strip,
  - Cut 4 **squares** $4^3/8$" x $4^3/8$". Cut a total of 16 squares.
- Cut 1 strip $4^1/2$" x 21". From this strip,
  - Cut 1 rectangle $4^1/2$" x 10". From this rectangle,
    - Cut 2 **block strips** $2^1/4$" x 10". Cut a total of 8 block strips.
  - Cut 2 **squares** $4^3/8$" x $4^3/8$". Cut a total of 8 squares. You will have 124 squares.
- Cut 4 strips $2^1/4$" x 21". From these strips,
  - Cut 4 **block strips** $2^1/4$" x 10". Cut a total of 16 block strips. You will have 124 block strips.
  - Cut 4 **narrow border strips** $2^1/4$" x 10". Cut a total of 16 narrow border strips. You will have 68 narrow border strips.

From cream print for setting triangles:
- Cut 2 strips 12" x the width of the fabric. From these strips,
  - Cut 5 squares 12" x 12". Cut squares *twice* diagonally to make 20 **side setting triangles**.
  - Cut 2 squares $6^1/2$" x $6^1/2$"". Cut squares *once* diagonally to make 4 **corner setting triangles**.

MAKING THE JEWEL BOX BLOCKS

*Follow **Piecing**, page 106, and **Pressing**, page 107, to assemble quilt top. Because there are so many seams in this quilt, you may need to use a seam allowance slightly smaller than the usual $1/4$". As you sew, measure your work to compare with the measurements provided and adjust your seam allowance as needed. Arrows on diagrams indicate suggested directions to press seam allowances.*

1. For **Jewel Box Block**, select 1 **square** and 1 **block strip** from 1 fabric and 1 **square** and 1 **block strip** from a contrasting fabric.
2. Draw a diagonal line (corner to corner) on wrong side of 1 square.

3. Matching right sides, place marked **square** on top of unmarked **square**. Stitch $1/4$" from each side of drawn line (**Fig. 1**). Cut along drawn line and press seam allowances to one side to make 2 **Triangle-Squares**. Triangle-Square should measure 4" x 4". Make 2 Triangle-Squares.

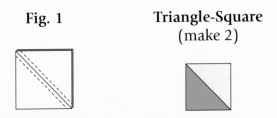

Fig. 1   **Triangle-Square** (make 2)

4. Sew 2 **block strips** together to make **Strip Set A**. Press seam allowances to one side. Strip Set A should measure 10" x 4". Cut across Strip Set A at $2^1/4$" intervals to make 4 **Unit 1's**. Unit 1 should measure $2^1/4$" x 4".

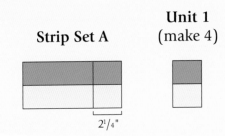

Strip Set A   **Unit 1** (make 4)

$2^1/4$"

5. Sew 2 **Unit 1's** together to make **Four Patch**. To press seam allowances, follow **Collapsing the Seams**, page 107. Four Patch should measure 4" x 4". Make 2 Four Patches.
6. Sew 1 **Four Patch** and 1 **Triangle-Square** together to make **Unit 2**. Make 2 Unit 2's.

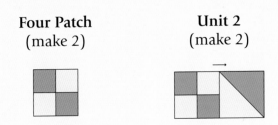

Four Patch (make 2)   **Unit 2** (make 2)

7. Sew 2 **Unit 2's** together to make **Jewel Box Block**. In the same manner as before, press seam allowances by "collapsing the seams." Block should measure $7^1/_2$" x $7^1/_2$".

8. Repeat **Steps 1–7** to make 61 Jewel Box Blocks. (If using fat quarters, you will have 2 squares and 2 block strips left over.)

Jewel Box Block (make 61)

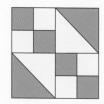

ASSEMBLING THE QUILT TOP CENTER

Refer to Assembly Diagram for placement.

1. Sew **Jewel Box Blocks** and **side setting triangles** together into diagonal **Rows**. Press seam allowances open or press them in one direction in every other Row and in the opposite direction in remaining Rows.

2. Sew **Rows** and **corner setting triangles** together to make quilt top center. Press seam allowances open or in one direction.

3. Trim quilt top center so that the corner seams (points) of the Blocks are $1/_2$" from the edge of the quilt top center. Quilt top center should measure approximately $60^1/_2$" x $60^1/_2$".

ADDING THE BORDERS

1. Sew 2 **wide border strips** together to make **Strip Set B**. Press seam allowances to one side. Strip Set B should measure 10" x 5". Make 4 Strip Set B's. Cut across Strip Set B's at $2^3/_4$" intervals to make 8 **Unit 3's**. Unit 3 should measure $2^3/_4$" x 5".

Strip Set B   **Unit 3**
(make 4)   (make 8)

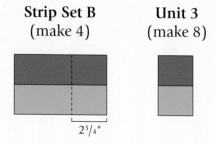

$2^3/_4$"

2. Sew 2 **Unit 3's** together to make **Corner Four Patch**. In the same manner as before, press seam allowances by "collapsing the seams." Corner Four Patch should measure 5" x 5". Make 4 Corner Four Patches.

Corner Four Patch (make 4)

3. Sew 34 **narrow border strips** together to make **Unit** 4. Press seam allowances open o in one direction. Make 2 Unit 4's.

Unit 4 (make 2)

4. Measure *length* across center of quilt top center. Measure length of 1 Unit 4. If measurements are not the same, make seams in Unit 4 slightly larger or smaller as needed.

5. Cut this Unit 4 in half (**Fig. 2**) to make 2 **side borders**. Do not sew side borders to quilt top center at this time.

Fig. 2

6. Measure *width* across center of quilt top center. Measure length of remaining Unit 4. If measurements are not the same, make seams in Unit 4 slightly larger or smaller as needed.

7. In the same manner as before, cut this Unit 4 in half to make 2 **top/bottom borders**. Do not sew top/bottom borders to quilt top center at this time.

3. Matching centers and corners, sew **side borders** to quilt top center. Press seam allowances to borders.

4. Sew 1 **Corner Four-Patch** to each end of **top/bottom borders**. Matching centers and corners, sew top/bottom borders to quilt top center. Press seam allowances to borders. Quilt top should measure approximately $69^1/2$" x $69^1/2$".

COMPLETING THE QUILT

1. To help stabilize the edges and prevent any seams from separating, stay-stitch around quilt top approximately $^1/8$" from the edge.

2. Follow **Machine Quilting**, page 107, to mark, layer, and quilt as desired. Quilt shown was machine meander quilted.

3. Follow **Making a Hanging Sleeve**, page 109, if a hanging sleeve is desired.

4. Cut a 26" square of binding fabric. Follow **Binding**, page 109, to bind quilt using 2"w bias binding with mitered corners.

Assembly Diagram

Looking GLASS

Quilted by Diane Tricka.

Finished Quilt Size:
78¹/₂" x 78¹/₂" (199 cm x 199 cm)
Finished Block Size:
6" x 6" (15 cm x 15 cm)

For this quilt, your only objective is to find a print you really love as a starting point. Whether it is soft and romantic, big and bold, or understated and elegant, the only important thing is that you love it. After that, it's just a matter of picking a background fabric and two colors for each nine patch.

The name of this quilt was chosen in a roundabout way. I was asked to donate a quilt to an auction in support of the fight against breast cancer. I always put a quotation on the back of my quilt, so this one had to be particularly inspirational. I used this one by Elisabeth Kübler-Ross, "People are like stained-glass windows. They sparkle and shine when the sun is out, but when the darkness sets in, their true beauty is revealed only if there is a light from within." When "Stained Glass" didn't really fit, my friend Sue suggested "Looking Glass." I think it fits.

Yardage Requirements

Yardage is based on 43"/44" (109 cm/113 cm) wide fabric. Fat quarters are approximately 21" x 18" (53 cm x 46 cm).

> 8 fat quarters of assorted pink prints
> 8 fat quarters of assorted brown prints
> $2^1/_4$ yds (2.1 m) of tan print fabric
> $1^1/_4$ yds (1.1 m) of cream print fabric
> $7^1/_4$ yds (6.6 m) of fabric for backing
> $^7/_8$ yd (80 cm) of fabric for binding

You will also need:

> 87" x 87" (221 cm x 221 cm) piece of batting

Cutting Out the Pieces

*Follow **Rotary Cutting**, page 105, to cut fabric. All measurements include $^1/_4$" seam allowances.*

From *each* assorted pink print fat quarter:
- Cut 5 **strips** $2^1/_2$" x 21". Cut a total of 39 strips.
- Cut 1 **border square** $2^1/_2$" x $2^1/_2$". Cut a total of 8 border squares.

From *each* assorted brown print fat quarter:
- Cut 7 **strips** $2^1/_2$" x 21". Cut a total of 56 strips.

From tan print fabric:
- Cut 2 strips $6^1/_2$" x the width of the fabric. From these strips,
  - Cut 8 **squares** $6^1/_2$" x $6^1/_2$".
  - Cut 6 **rectangles** $6^1/_2$" x $4^1/_2$".
- Cut 6 strips $6^1/_2$" x the width of the fabric. From these strips,
  - Cut 46 **rectangles** $6^1/_2$" x $4^1/_2$". You will have 52 rectangles.
- Cut 8 **border strips** $2^1/_2$" x the width of the fabric.

From cream print fabric:
- Cut 16 strips $2^1/_2$" x width of fabric. Cut each strip in half to make 32 **strips**.

Making the Nine Patch Blocks

*Follow **Piecing**, page 106, and **Pressing**, page 107, to assemble quilt top. Because there are so many seams in this quilt, you may need to use a seam allowance slightly smaller than the usual $^1/_4$". As you sew, measure your work to compare with the measurements provided, which include seam allowances, and adjust your seam allowance as needed. Arrows on diagrams indicate suggested directions to press seam allowances.*

1. Sew 2 matching brown **strips** and 1 cream **strip** together to make **Strip Set A**. Strip Set A should measure 21" x $6^1/_2$". Make 16 Strip Set A's. Cut across Strip Set A's at $2^1/_2$" intervals to make 128 **Unit 1's**. Unit 1 should measure $2^1/_2$" x $6^1/_2$".

Strip Set A (make 16)   **Unit 1** (make 128)

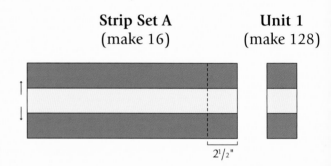

2. Sew 2 cream **strips** and 1 pink **strip** together to make **Strip Set B**. Strip Set B should measure 21" x $6^1/_2$". Make 8 Strip Set B's. Cut across Strip Set B's at $2^1/_2$" intervals to make 61 **Unit 2's**. Unit 2 should measure $2^1/_2$" x $6^1/_2$".

Strip Set B (make 8)   **Unit 2** (make 61)

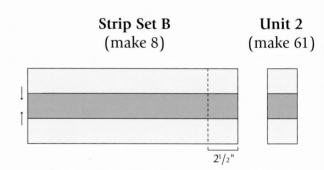

Sew 2 matching **Unit 1's** and 1 **Unit 2** together to make **Nine Patch Block**. Nine Patch should measure $6^1/2$" x $6^1/2$". Make 61 Nine Patch Blocks. Set aside left over Unit 1's for outer border.

Nine Patch Block (make 61)

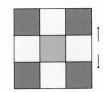

MAKING THE ALTERNATING BLOCKS

The Alternating Blocks are made in sets of four matching Blocks. Each set of four Alternating Blocks coordinates with one of the Nine Patch Blocks – the pink and brown fabrics in the Nine Patch Blocks and the Alternating Blocks are the same.

1. Select 13 Nine Patch Blocks. For each selected Nine Patch Block, select 1 pink **strip** and 1 brown **strip** that match the pink and brown prints in the Nine Patch Block. Cut both strips in half so that each yields 2 **short strips** $2^1/2$" x $10^1/2$".

2. Sew 2 matching pink **short strips** and 1 brown **short strip** together to make **Strip Set C**. (Set aside left over brown short strip for outer border.) Strip Set C should measure $10^1/2$" x $6^1/2$". Cut across Strip Set C at $2^1/2$" intervals to make 4 **Unit 3's**. Unit 3 should measure $2^1/2$" x $6^1/2$".

Strip Set C

Unit 3 (make 4)

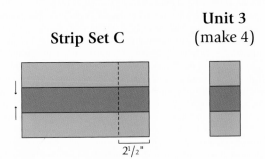

$2^1/2$"

3. Sew 1 **Unit 3** and 1 **rectangle** together to make **Alternating Block**. Alternating Block should measure $6^1/2$" x $6^1/2$". Make 4 matching Alternating Blocks.

4. Repeat **Steps 2–3** to make 13 sets of 4 matching Alternating Blocks.

Alternating Block (make 13 sets of 4 matching)

ASSEMBLING THE QUILT TOP CENTER

1. Refer to **Assembly Diagram**, page 93, to sew **Nine Patch Blocks**, **Alternating Blocks**, and **squares** into **Rows**. Press seam allowances open or to Alternating Blocks and squares.

2. Sew Rows together to complete quilt top center. Press seam allowances open or in one direction. Quilt top center should measure $66^1/2$" x $66^1/2$".

ADDING THE INNER BORDER

1. Using diagonal seams (**Fig. 1**), sew **border strips** together into a continuous strip. Press seam allowances open.

Fig. 1

2. To determine length of **side inner borders**, measure *length* across center of quilt top center. Cut 2 side inner borders from continuous strip. Matching centers and corners, sew side inner borders to quilt top center. Press seam allowances to borders.

3. To determine length of **top/bottom inner borders**, measure *width* across center of quilt top center (including added borders). Cut 2 top/bottom inner borders from continuous strip. Matching centers and corners, sew top/bottom inner borders to quilt top center. Press seam allowances to borders.

ADDING THE OUTER BORDER

1. Select 11 brown strips and 11 pink strips. Sew 1 brown strip and 1 pink strip together to make **Strip Set D**. Strip Set D should measure 21" x 4$^1/_2$". Make 11 Strip Set D's. Set Strip Set D's aside.

Strip Set D (make 11)

2. Select 7 pink strips and cut them in half to make 14 **short strips** 2$^1/_2$" x 10$^1/_2$".

3. Sew 1 pink **short strip** and 1 brown **short strip** together to make **Strip Set E**. Strip Set E should measure 10$^1/_2$" x 4$^1/_2$". Make 13 Strip Set E's. (You will have 1 pink short strip left over.)

Strip Set E (make 13)

4. Cut across Strip Set D's and Strip Set E's at 2$^1/_2$" intervals to make 140 **Unit 4's**. Unit 4 should measure 2$^1/_2$" x 4$^1/_2$". As you cut, make 4 stacks with 2 Unit 4's from each Strip Set D and 1 Unit 4 from each Strip Set E in each stack. You should have 4 stacks of 35 Unit 4's each.

Unit 4 (make 140)

5. Using the leftover Unit 1's set aside earlier, remove seams to get 8 brown **border squares**.

6. Sew 1 brown **border square** and 1 pink **border square** together to make **Unit 5**. Unit 5 should measure 2$^1/_2$" x 4$^1/_2$". Make 8 Unit 5's.

Unit 5 (make 8)

7. Sew 35 **Unit 4's** (1 stack) together to make **side outer border**. Make 2 side outer borders. Press seam allowances in one direction. Measure *length* across center of quilt top. Measure length of side outer borders. If measurements are not the same, make seams in borders slightly larger or smaller as needed. Matching center and corners, sew side outer borders to quilt top. Press seam allowances to outer borders.

8. Sew 35 **Unit 4's** (1 stack) and 4 **Unit 5's** together to make **top outer border**. Press seam allowances in one direction. Repeat to make **bottom outer border**. Measure *width* across center of quilt top (including added borders). Measure length of top/bottom outer borders. If measurements are not the same, make seams in borders slightly larger or smaller as needed. Matching centers and corners, sew top/bottom borders to quilt top. Press seam allowances to outer borders. Quilt top should measure 78$^1/_2$" x 78$^1/_2$".

COMPLETING THE QUILT

. To help stabilize the edges and prevent any seams from separating, stay-stitch around quilt top approximately $^1/_8$" from the edge.

. Follow **Machine Quilting**, page 107, to mark, layer, and quilt as desired. Quilt shown was machine quilted. A small design or an "X" was quilted in each small square of the Blocks. Circular feather patterns were quilted in the tan print areas. A leaf pattern was quilted in the inner border, and the outer border was crosshatch quilted.

3. Follow **Making a Hanging Sleeve**, page 109, if a hanging sleeve is desired.

4. Cut a 28" square of binding fabric. Follow **Binding**, page 109, to bind quilt using 2"w bias binding with mitered corners.

NOTE: For a quilt measuring 90" x 90", make 85 Nine Patch Blocks, 72 Alternating Blocks (18 sets of 4 matching) and 12 plain squares. The outer borders will require 172 Unit 4's (344 squares).

Assembly Diagram

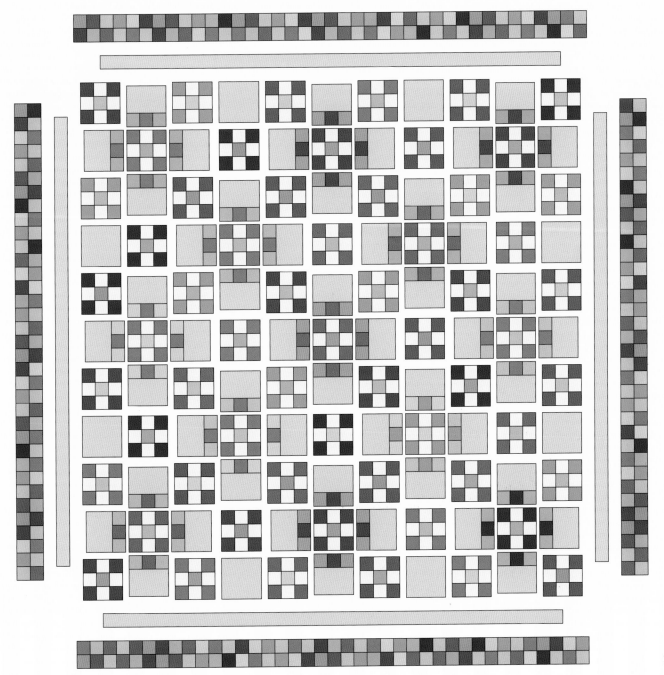

Crackling PALMS

DIAGONAL SETTING

Quilted by Diane Tricka.

Finished Quilt Size:
71⁵/₈" x 82¹/₄" (182 cm x 209 cm)
Finished Block Size:
7¹/₂" x 7¹/₂" (19 cm x 19 cm)

What's not to love about the Crackling Palm block? All you need is a "lighter" fabric and a "darker" fabric, and any kind of fabric or color palette will work. The quilt is perfect for fat quarters. After you piece the parts of the block, you get to decide whether you want the block to have a light or dark background. So why did I make this quilt with the blocks on point and again with the blocks straight set (page 100)? Two reasons: because it looks so different and each quilt uses the same number of blocks. This may actually be the perfect block!

The unusual name of this quilt came about because I thought the block looked like fireworks— the kind of firecracker that spins and sparkles. The problem was, I didn't know what these firecrackers were called.

So I called an expert. My brother Mark knows all kinds of really cool things. He found Web sites that sell fireworks and—Bingo!—I have a quilt name I absolutely love. Now if I can just get a couple of those firecrackers….

95

YARDAGE REQUIREMENTS

Yardage is based on 43"/44" (109 cm/112 cm) wide fabric. Fat quarters are approximately 21" x 18" (53 cm x 46 cm).

  31 fat quarters of assorted dark print, medium print, and light print fabrics
  1 yd (91 cm) of red/tan check fabric
  ⁷/₈ yd (80 cm) of fabric for binding
  6³/₄ yds (6.2 m)* of fabric for backing

You will also need:

  80" x 90" (203 cm x 229 cm) piece of batting
  Small square acrylic ruler (4" or larger)
  Template plastic
  Permanent marker

  *Yardage is based on three 80" (203 cm) lengths of fabric, which allows for a larger backing for long arm quilting. If you are using another quilting method, two 90" (229 cm) lengths or 5 yds (4.6 m), will be adequate.

CUTTING OUT THE PIECES

*Follow **Rotary Cutting**, page 105, to cut fabric. All measurements include ¹/₄" seam allowances. Side and corner setting triangles are slightly larger than needed and will be trimmed. Small and large rectangles are used in the Blocks and border. You will cut extra rectangles so that you will have options for making the border.*

From *each* assorted fat quarter:

- Cut 1 strip 6" x 21". From this strip,
  - Cut 11 **large rectangles** 1³/₄" x 6". Cut a total of 341 (144 sets of 2 matching and 53 assorted) large rectangles.
- Cut 2 strips 4¹/₄" x 21". From these strips,
  - Cut 22 **small rectangles** 1³/₄" x 4¹/₄". Cut a total of 682 small rectangles.
- Cut 1 strip 1³/₄" x 21". From this strip,
  - Cut 4 **small rectangles** 1³/₄" x 4¹/₄". Cut a total of 124 assorted small rectangles. You will have 806 (144 sets of 4 matching and 230 assorted) small rectangles.

From red/tan check fabric:

- Cut 2 strips 12" by the width of the fabric. From these strips,
  - Cut 6 squares 12" x 12". Cut squares *twice* diagonally to make 24 **side setting triangles**. (You will use 22 and have 2 left over.)
- Cut 2 squares 6¹/₂" x 6¹/₂". Cut squares *once* diagonally to make 4 **corner setting triangles**.

MAKING THE CUTTING GUIDE

This cutting guide will make cutting the diagonal lines in the Blocks and borders quicker and easier.

1. For template, cut a rectangle from template plastic 1³/₄" x 6". Using permanent marker, mark rectangle as shown (**Fig. 1**). Cut along drawn line; discard 1 piece.

Fig. 1

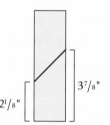

Template

2. Using clear tape and making sure template is turned as shown, tape template to bottom of small square ruler to make cutting guide.

Cutting Guide

MAKING THE BLOCKS

Follow **Piecing**, page 106, and **Pressing**, page 107, to assemble quilt top. Because there are so many seams in this quilt, you may need to use a seam allowance slightly smaller than the usual $1/4$". As you sew, measure your work to compare with the measurements provided and adjust your seam allowance as needed. Arrows on diagrams indicate suggested directions to press seam allowances.

. For **Block**, select 2 **large rectangles** and 4 **small rectangles** from *each* of 2 contrasting fabrics.

. Placing cutting guide over end of large rectangle and cutting along edge of ruler (**Fig. 2**), cut **large rectangle** in half to make 2 **segments**. Make 8 **segments**.

Fig. 2

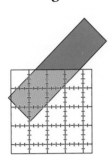

Segment (make 8)

. Sew 2 contrasting **segments** together as shown in **Fig. 3** to make **pieced rectangle**. Press seam allowances open. Trim pieced rectangle to $1^3/4$" x $4^1/4$" as shown. Make 4 pieced rectangles.

Fig. 3

Pieced Rectangle (make 4)

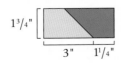

$1^3/4$"

3"　$1^1/4$"

4. Sew 2 contrasting **small rectangles** and 1 **pieced rectangle** together to make **Unit 1**. Unit 1 should measure $4^1/4$" x $4^1/4$". Make 4 Unit 1's.

Unit 1 (make 4)

5. Sew 2 **Unit 1's** together to make **Unit 2**. Make 2 Unit 2's.

Unit 2 (make 2)

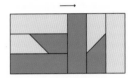

6. Sew 2 **Unit 2's** together to make **Block**. To press seam allowances, follow **Collapsing the Seams**, page 107. Block should measure 8" x 8".

7. Follow **Steps 1–6** to make a total of 72 Blocks.

Block (make 72)

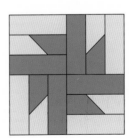

ASSEMBLING THE QUILT TOP CENTER

Refer to Assembly Diagram for placement.

1. Sew **Blocks** and **side setting triangles** together into diagonal **Rows**. Press seam allowances open or press them in one direction in every other Row and in the opposite direction in remaining Rows.
2. Sew **Rows** together, pressing seam allowances open or in one direction.
3. Sew **corner setting triangles** to quilt top center. Press seam allowances open or to corner setting triangles.
4. Trim quilt top center so that corner seams (points) of Blocks are $1/4$" from edge of quilt top center. Quilt top center should measure approximately $64^1/8$" x $74^3/4$".

ADDING THE BORDERS

Refer to Quilt Top Diagram for placement.

1. Sew 3 **large rectangles** together to make **Strip Set**. Strip set should measure 6" x $4^1/4$". Make 4 Strip Sets. (For more variety, make more Strip Sets.) Cut across Strip Sets at $1^3/4$" intervals to make 12 **Unit 3's**. Unit 3 should measure $1^3/4$" x $4^1/4$".

Strip Set (make 4) **Unit 3** (make 12)

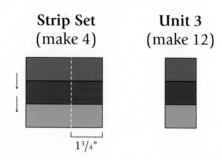

$1^3/4$"

2. Sew 3 **Unit 3's** together to make **Nine Patch**. Nine Patch should measure $4^1/4$" x $4^1/4$". Make 4 Nine Patches.

Nine Patch (make 4)

3. *Note: For borders, you may use small rectangles only, or you may include as many pieced rectangles as you like.* For each **pieced rectangle**, use 2 contrasting **large rectangles** and follow **Steps 2–3** of **Making the Blocks**.
4. Sew a total of 60 **small rectangles** and **pieced rectangles** together to make **side border**. Press seam allowances open or in one direction. Make 2 side borders. Measure *length* across center of quilt top center. Measure length of side borders. If measurements are not the same, make seams in borders slightly larger or smaller as needed. Do not sew side borders to quilt top center at this time.
5. Sew a total of 51 **small rectangles** and **pieced rectangles** together to make **top border**. Press seam allowances open or in one direction. Repeat to make **bottom border**. Measure *width* across center of quilt top center. Measure length of top/bottom borders. If measurements are not the same, make seams in borders slightly larger or smaller as needed. Sew 1 **Nine Patch** to each end of each top/bottom border. Do not sew top/bottom borders to quilt top center at this time.
6. Matching centers and corners, sew **side** and then **top** and **bottom borders** to quilt top center. Press seam allowances to borders. Quilt top should measure approximately $71^5/8$" x $82^1/4$".

Assembly Diagram

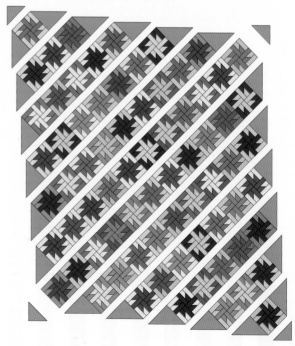

COMPLETING THE QUILT

1. To help stabilize the edges and prevent any seams from separating, stay-stitch around quilt top approximately ⅛" from the edge.
2. Follow **Machine Quilting**, page 107, to mark, layer, and quilt as desired. Quilt shown was machine quilted with feather patterns in the Block centers and flower patterns in the outer portions of the Blocks. Straight crisscrossing lines were quilted in the setting triangles and overlapping arches were quilted in the borders. An "X" was quilted in each square of the Nine Patches.

3. Follow **Making a Hanging Sleeve**, page 109, if a hanging sleeve is desired.
4. Cut a 27" square of binding fabric. Follow **Binding**, page 109, to bind quilt using 2"w bias binding with mitered corners.

NOTE: This quilt can be made larger or smaller by adding or subtracting diagonal Rows. Each Row will change the measurement of the quilt by approximately 10⅝".

Quilt Top Diagram

Crackling
PALMS
STRAIGHT SETTING

Pieced by Judy Adams.
Quilted by Louise Haley.

Finished Quilt Size:
70$^1/_2$" x 78" (179 cm x 198 cm)
Finished Block Size:
7$^1/_2$" x 7$^1/_2$" (19 cm x 19 cm)

Look at the straight setting of Crackling Palms blocks on this quilt, then look at the diagonal setting in the quilt on page 94. See the difference? The same block takes on a different look when placed in a straight setting. And again, you can wait until you put the four sections of each block together before you decide if it's a light-on-dark block or a dark-on-light block. Fun stuff!

YARDAGE REQUIREMENTS

Yardage is based on 43"/44" (109 cm/112 cm) wide fabric. Fat quarters are approximately 21" x 18" (53 cm x 46 cm).

31 fat quarters of assorted dark print, medium print, and light print fabrics

$3/8$ yd (34 cm) of tan print fabric

$7/8$ yd (80 cm) of fabric for binding

$4^7/8$ yds (4.5 m) of fabric for backing

You will also need:

79" x 86" (201 cm x 218 cm) piece of batting

Small square acrylic ruler (4" or larger)

Template plastic

Permanent marker

CUTTING OUT THE PIECES

*Follow **Rotary Cutting**, page 105, to cut fabric. All measurements include $1/4$" seam allowances. Small and large rectangles are used in the Blocks and border. You will cut extra rectangles so that you will have options for making the outer border.*

From *each* assorted fat quarter:

- Cut 1 strip 6" x 21". From this strip,
  - Cut 11 **large rectangles** $1^3/4$" x 6". Cut a total of 341 (144 sets of 2 matching and 53 assorted) large rectangles.
- Cut 2 strips $4^1/4$" x 21". From these strips,
  - Cut 22 **small rectangles** $1^3/4$" x $4^1/4$". Cut a total of 682 small rectangles.
- Cut 1 strip $1^3/4$" x 21". From this strip,
  - Cut 4 **small rectangles** $1^3/4$" x $4^1/4$". Cut a total of 124 assorted small rectangles. You will have 806 (144 sets of 4 matching and 230 assorted) small rectangles.

From tan print fabric:

- Cut 7 **border strips** $1^3/4$" by the width of the fabric.

MAKING THE BLOCKS

1. Make 72 **Blocks** following **Making the Cutting Guide** and **Making the Blocks** from the Crackling Palms Diagonal Setting Quilt, pages 96–97.

Block (make 72)

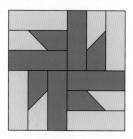

ASSEMBLING THE QUILT TOP CENTER

*Refer to **Quilt Top Diagram**, page 104, for placement.*

1. Sew 8 **Blocks** together to make **Row**. Press seam allowances open or press them in one direction in every other Row and in the opposite direction in remaining Rows. Make 9 Rows.
2. Sew **Rows** together, pressing seam allowances open or in one direction. Quilt top center should measure $60^1/2$" x 68".

ADDING THE INNER BORDER

1. Using diagonal seams (**Fig. 1**), sew **border strips** together into a continuous strip. Press seam allowances open.

Fig. 1

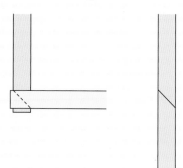

- To determine length of **side inner borders**, measure *length* across center of quilt top center. Cut 2 side inner borders from continuous strip. Matching centers and corners, sew side inner borders to quilt top center. Press seam allowances to borders.
- To determine length of **top/bottom inner borders**, measure *width* across center of quilt top center (including added borders). Cut 2 top/bottom inner borders from continuous strip. Matching centers and corners, sew top/bottom inner borders to quilt top center. Press seam allowances to borders.

ADDING THE OUTER BORDER

Note: For outer borders, you may use small rectangles only, or you may include as many pieced rectangles and three-square rectangles as you like.

1. For each **pieced rectangle**, use 2 contrasting **large rectangles** and follow **Steps 2–3** of **Making the Blocks** from the Crackling Palms Diagonal Setting Quilt, page 97. Pieced rectangle should measure $1^3/_4$" x $4^1/_4$".

Pieced Rectangle

2. For each **three-square rectangles**, cut 3 squares $1^3/_4$" x $1^3/_4$" from small or large rectangles or leftover scraps; sew squares together. Three-square rectangle should measure $1^3/_4$" x $4^1/_4$". Make at least 12 three-square rectangles for corner Nine Patches.

Three-Square Rectangle (make at least 12)

3. Sew 3 **three-square rectangles** together to make **Nine Patch**. Nine Patch should measure $4^1/_4$" x $4^1/_4$". Make 4 Nine Patches.

Nine Patch (make 4)

4. Sew a total of 56 **small rectangles**, **pieced rectangles**, and **three-square rectangles** together to make **side outer border**. Press seam allowances open or in one direction. Make 2 side outer borders. Measure *length* across center of quilt top. Measure length of side outer borders. If measurements are not the same, make seams in borders slightly larger or smaller as needed. Do not sew side outer borders to quilt top at this time.

5. Sew a total of 50 **small rectangles**, **pieced rectangles**, and **three-square rectangles** together to make **top outer border**. Press seam allowances open or in one direction. Repeat to make **bottom outer border**. Measure *width* across center of quilt top. Measure length of top/bottom outer borders. If measurements are not the same, make seams in borders slightly larger or smaller as needed. Sew 1 **Nine Patch** to each end of each top/bottom outer border. Do not sew top/bottom outer borders to quilt top at this time.

6. Matching centers and corners, sew **side** and then **top** and **bottom outer borders** to quilt top. Press seam allowances to outer borders. Quilt top should measure $70^1/_2$" x 78".

COMPLETING THE QUILT

1. To help stabilize the edges and prevent any seams from separating, stay-stitch around the quilt top approximately $1/8$" from the edge.
2. Follow **Machine Quilting**, page 107, to mark, layer, and quilt as desired. Quilt shown was machine quilted with flower patterns in the Blocks, loops in the inner border, zigzag lines in the outer border, and curved lines in each square of the Nine Patches

3. Follow **Making a Hanging Sleeve**, page 109, if a hanging sleeve is desired.
4. Cut a 27" square of binding fabric. Follow **Binding**, page 109, to bind quilt using 2"w bias binding with mitered corners.

NOTE: This quilt can be made larger or smaller by adding or subtracting horizontal Rows or vertical Rows. Each Row will change the measurement of the quilt by $7^1/2$".

Quilt Top Diagram

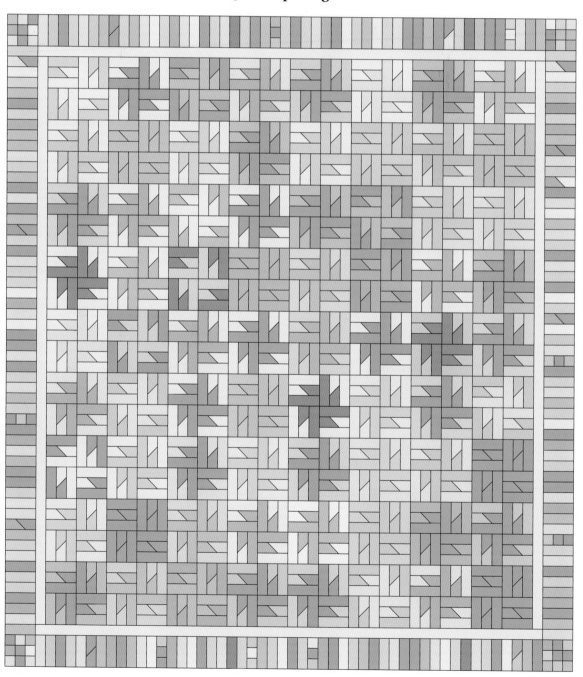

General
INSTRUCTIONS

To make your quilting easier and more enjoyable, we encourage you to carefully read all of the general instructions, study the color photographs, and familiarize yourself with the individual project instructions before beginning a project.

FABRICS

SELECTING FABRICS

Choose high-quality, medium-weight 100% cotton fabrics. All-cotton fabrics hold a crease better, fray less, and are easier to quilt than cotton/polyester blends.

Yardage requirements listed for each project are based on 43"/44" wide fabric with a "usable" width of 40" after shrinkage and trimming selvages. Actual usable width will probably vary slightly from fabric to fabric. Our recommended yardage lengths should be adequate for occasional re-squaring of fabric when many cuts are required.

While the size of fat quarters may vary slightly, each should be at least 21" x 18" (53 cm x 46 cm). If they are smaller, more fat quarters may be required.

PREPARING FABRICS

Pre-washing fabrics may cause edges to ravel. As a result, your fat quarters and other pre-cut fabric pieces may not be large enough to cut all of the pieces required for your chosen project. Therefore, we do not recommend pre-washing your yardage or pre-cut fabrics. Refer to **Caring for Your Quilt**, page 112, for instructions on washing your finished quilt.

Before cutting, prepare fabrics with a steam iron set on cotton and starch or sizing (such as Best Press™ Sizing/Clear Starch Alternative). The starch or sizing will give the fabric a crisp finish. This will make cutting more accurate and may make piecing easier.

ROTARY CUTTING

Rotary cutting has brought speed and accuracy to quiltmaking by allowing quilters to easily cut strips of fabric and then cut those strips into smaller pieces. It is helpful to keep pieces separated and identified in zip top bags.
***Note:** Most measurements provided in this book are exact. Many quilters prefer to "over-cut" triangles or squares which will be sewn and cut into triangles (as in Triangle-Squares, Flying Geese, or Hourglasses) and then trimming them to exact size after sewing. If you choose to over-cut, you may need additional fabric.*

CUTTING FROM FAT QUARTERS

- Place fabric flat on work surface with lengthwise (18") edge closest to you.
- Cut all strips parallel to 21" edge of the fabric unless otherwise indicated in project instructions.
- To cut each strip required for a project, place ruler over left edge of fabric, aligning desired marking on ruler with left edge; make cut.

CUTTING FROM YARDAGE

- Place fabric yardage on work surface with fold closest to you.
- Cut all strips from the selvage-to-selvage width of the fabric unless otherwise indicated in project instructions.
- Square left edge of fabric using rotary cutter and rulers (**Figs. 1 – 2**).

Fig. 1

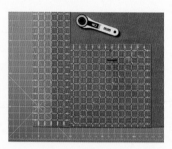

Fig. 2

- To cut each strip required for a project, place ruler over cut edge of fabric, aligning desired marking on ruler with cut edge; make cut (**Fig. 3**).

Fig. 3

- When cutting several strips from a single piece of fabric, it is important to make sure that cuts remain at a perfect right angle to the fold; square fabric as needed.

PIECING

Precise cutting, followed by accurate piecing, will ensure that all pieces of quilt top fit together well.

- Set sewing machine stitch length for approximately 11 stitches per inch.
- Use neutral-colored general-purpose sewing thread (not quilting thread) in needle and in bobbin.

- A consistent seam allowance is *essential*. Because there are so many seams in each of the quilts in this book, you many need to use a seam allowance slightly smaller than the usual $1/4$". As you sew, measure your work to compare with the measurements provided in the project instructions and adjust your seam allowance as needed. Presser feet that are $1/4$" wide are available for most sewing machines.
- When piecing, always place pieces right sides together and match raw edges; pin if necessary.
- Chain piecing saves time and will usually result in more accurate piecing.
- Trim away points of seam allowances that extend beyond edges of sewn pieces.

SEWING STRIP SETS

When there are several strips to assemble into a strip set, first sew strips together into pairs, then sew pairs together to form strip set. To help avoid distortion, sew seams in opposite directions (**Fig. 4**).

Fig. 4

SEWING ACROSS SEAM INTERSECTIONS

When sewing across intersection of two seams, place pieces right sides together and match seams exactly, making sure seam allowances are pressed in opposite directions (**Fig. 5**).

SEWING SHARP POINTS

To ensure sharp points when joining triangular or diagonal pieces, stitch across the center of the "X" (shown in pink) formed on wrong side by previous seams (**Fig. 6**).

Fig. 5

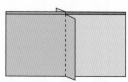

Fig. 6

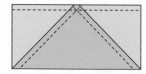

PRESSING

For years, hand quilters have pressed seam allowances to one side to prevent seams from pulling open. Since most of us now use sewing machines, the stitches are smaller and tighter. Also, the fabrics, thread, and batting we use today are better quality. Consequently, we have fewer concerns about any weaknesses that might arise when seam allowances are pressed open. Pressing seam allowances open may make points sharper and will result in less bulk when adjacent points are joined. However, pressing the seams open may make quilting in the ditch more difficult. In the end, it is entirely a personal choice.

- Use steam iron set on "Cotton" for all pressing.
- Press after sewing each seam.
- Suggestions for pressing seam allowances are provided with each project.
- To prevent dark fabric seam allowance from showing through light fabric, trim darker seam allowance slightly narrower than lighter seam allowance.
- To press long seams, such as those in long strip sets, without curving or other distortion, lay strips across width of the ironing board.

COLLAPSING THE SEAMS

When pressing where 2 seams intersect, such as the center of a Four Patch, "collapsing the seams" will reduce bulk. To collapse the seam, use a seam ripper to remove the stitches that are in the seam allowances of the seam just made (**Fig. 7**). Press seam allowances clockwise or counter clockwise. At the seam intersection, press the seam allowances open so that the center lies flat (**Fig. 8**).

Fig. 7

Fig. 8

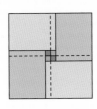

MACHINE QUILTING

Quilting holds the three layers (top, batting, and backing) of the quilt together. Because marking, layering, and quilting are interrelated and may be done in different orders depending on circumstances, please read entire **Machine Quilting** section, pages 107–109, before beginning project.

MARKING QUILTING LINES

Quilting lines may be marked using fabric marking pencils, chalk markers, or water- or air-soluble pens.

Simple quilting designs may be marked with chalk or chalk pencil after basting. A small area may be marked, then quilted, before moving to next area to be marked. Intricate designs should be marked before basting using a more durable marker.

Caution: Pressing may permanently set some marks. **Test** different markers **on scrap fabric** to find one that marks clearly and can be thoroughly removed.

A wide variety of pre-cut quilting stencils, as well as entire books of quilting patterns, are available. Using a stencil makes it easier to mark intricate or repetitive designs.

To make a stencil from a pattern, center template plastic over pattern and use a permanent marker to trace pattern onto plastic. Use a craft knife with single or double blade to cut channels along traced lines (**Fig. 9**).

Fig. 9

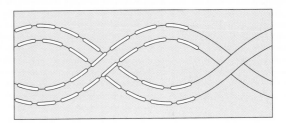

PREPARING THE BACKING

To allow for slight shifting of quilt top during quilting, backing should be approximately 4" larger on all sides. Yardage requirements listed for quilt backings are calculated for 43"/44"w fabric. Using 90"w or 108"w fabric for the backing of a quilt may eliminate piecing. To piece a backing using 43"/44"w fabric, use the following instructions.

1. Measure length and width of quilt top; add 8" to each measurement.
2. **If determined width is 79" or less**, cut backing fabric into two lengths slightly longer than determined *length* measurement. Trim selvages. Place lengths with right sides facing and sew long edges together, forming tube (**Fig. 10**). Match seams and press along one fold (**Fig. 11**). Cut along pressed fold to form single piece (**Fig. 12**).

Fig. 10	**Fig. 11**	**Fig. 12**

3. **If determined width is more than 79"**, it may require less fabric yardage if the backing is pieced horizontally. Divide determined *length* measurement by 40" to determine how many widths will be needed. Cut required number of widths the determined *width* measurement. Trim selvages. Sew long edges together to form single piece.
4. Trim backing to size determined in Step 1; press seam allowances open.

CHOOSING THE BATTING

The appropriate batting will make quilting easier. All cotton or cotton/polyester blend battings work well for machine quilting because the cotton helps "grip" quilt layers.

Types of batting include cotton, polyester, wool, cotton/polyester blend, cotton/wool blend, and silk.

When selecting batting, refer to package labels for characteristics and care instructions. Cut batting same size as prepared backing.

ASSEMBLING THE QUILT

1. Examine wrong side of quilt top closely; trim any seam allowances and clip any threads that may show through front of the quilt. Press quilt top, being careful not to "set" any marked quilting lines.
2. Place backing *wrong* side up on flat surface. Use masking tape to tape edges of backing to surface. Place batting on top of backing fabric. Smooth batting gently, being careful not to stretch or tear. Center quilt top *right* side up on batting.
3. Use 1" rustproof safety pins to "pin-baste" all layers together, spacing pins approximately 4" apart. Begin at center and work toward outer edges to secure all layers. If possible, place pins away from areas that will be quilted, although pins may be removed as needed when quilting.

QUILTING METHODS

Use general-purpose thread in bobbin. Do not use quilting thread. Thread the needle of machine with general-purpose thread or transparent monofilament thread to make quilting blend with quilt top fabrics. Use decorative thread, such as a metallic or contrasting-color general-purpose thread, to make quilting lines stand out more.

Straight-Line Quilting

The term "straight-line" is somewhat deceptive, since curves (especially gentle ones) as well as straight lines can be stitched with this technique.

1. Set stitch length for 6 to 10 stitches per inch and attach walking foot to sewing machine.
2. Determine which section of quilt will have longest continuous quilting line, oftentimes area from center top to center bottom. Roll up and secure each edge of quilt to help reduce the bulk, keeping fabrics smooth.

- Begin stitching on longest quilting line, using very short stitches for the first $1/4$" to "lock" quilting. Stitch across quilt, using one hand on each side of walking foot to slightly spread fabric and to guide fabric through machine. Lock stitches at end of quilting line.
- Continue machine quilting, stitching longer quilting lines first to stabilize quilt before moving on to other areas.

Free-Motion Quilting

Free-motion quilting may be free form or may follow a marked pattern.

- Attach darning foot to sewing machine and lower or cover feed dogs.
- Position quilt under darning foot; lower foot. Holding top thread, take a stitch and pull bobbin thread to top of quilt. To "lock" beginning of quilting line, hold top and bobbin threads while making 3 to 5 stitches in place.
- Use one hand on each side of darning foot to slightly spread fabric and to move fabric through the machine. Even stitch length is achieved by using smooth, flowing hand motion and steady machine speed. Slow machine speed and fast hand movement will create long stitches. Fast machine speed and slow hand movement will create short stitches. Move quilt sideways, back and forth, in a circular motion, or in a random motion to create desired designs; do not rotate quilt. Lock stitches at end of each quilting line.

MAKING A HANGING SLEEVE

Attaching a hanging sleeve to the back of a quilt before the binding is added allows your quilt to be displayed on a wall.

- Measure width of quilt top edge and subtract 1". Cut piece of fabric 7"w by determined measurement.
- Press short edges of fabric piece $1/4$" to wrong side; press edges $1/4$" to wrong side again and machine stitch in place.
- Matching wrong sides, fold piece in half lengthwise to form tube.

4. Follow project instructions to sew binding to quilt top and to trim backing and batting. Before Blindstitching binding to backing, match raw edges and stitch hanging sleeve to center top edge on back of quilt.
5. Finish binding quilt, treating hanging sleeve as part of backing.
6. Blindstitch bottom of hanging sleeve to backing, taking care not to stitch through to front of quilt.
7. Insert dowel or slat into hanging sleeve.

BINDING

MAKING CONTINUOUS BIAS STRIP BINDING
Bias strips for binding can simply be cut and pieced to desired length. However, when a long length of binding is needed, the "continuous" method is quick and accurate.

1. Cut square from binding fabric the size indicated in project instructions. Cut square in half diagonally to make two triangles.
2. With right sides together and using $1/4$" seam allowance, sew triangles together (**Fig. 13**); press seam allowances open.
3. On wrong side of fabric, draw lines the width of binding as specified in project instructions, usually 2" (**Fig. 14**). Cut off any remaining fabric less than this width.

Fig. 13   **Fig. 14**

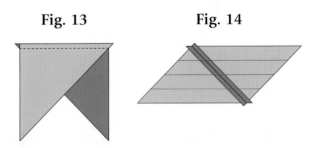

4. With right sides inside, bring short edges together to form tube; match raw edges so that first drawn line of top section meets second drawn line of bottom section (**Fig. 15**).

Fig. 15

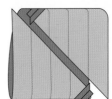

5. Carefully pin edges together by inserting pins through drawn lines at point where drawn lines intersect, making sure pins go through intersections on both sides. Using $1/4$" seam allowance, sew edges together; press seam allowances open.

6. To cut continuous strip, begin cutting along first drawn line (**Fig. 16**). Continue cutting along drawn line around tube.

Fig. 16

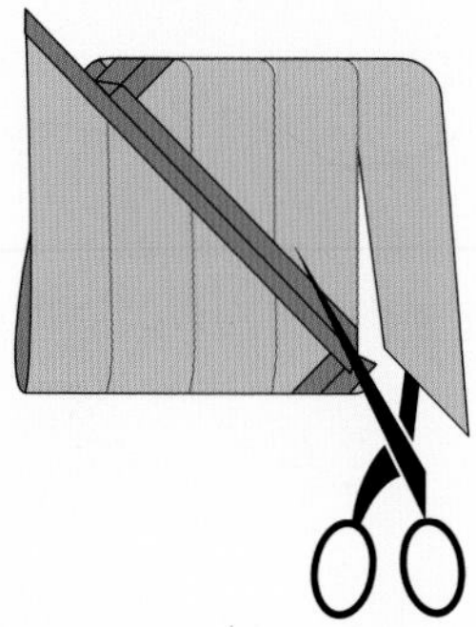

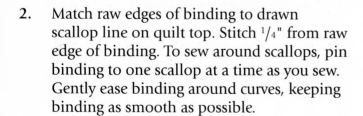

7. Trim ends of bias strip square.
8. Matching wrong sides and raw edges, carefully press bias strip in half lengthwise to complete binding.

ATTACHING BINDING ON SCALLOPED-EDGED QUILTS

After the quilting is complete, attach the binding before trimming the edges of the quilt as it will help keep the edge from stretching or bunching up.
1. Press one end of binding diagonally (**Fig. 17**).

Fig. 17

2. Match raw edges of binding to drawn scallop line on quilt top. Stitch $1/4$" from raw edge of binding. To sew around scallops, pin binding to one scallop at a time as you sew. Gently ease binding around curves, keeping binding as smooth as possible.

3. Continue sewing binding to quilt until binding overlaps beginning end by approximately 2". Trim excess binding.
4. Trim quilt top, batting, and backing $1/4$" from stitching line, even with binding seam allowances.
5. Fold binding over to quilt backing and pin pressed edge in place covering stitching line.
6. Blindstitch (**Fig. 30**, page 112) binding to backing, taking care not to stitch through to front of quilt.

ATTACHING BINDING WITH MITERED CORNERS

1. Beginning with one end near center on bottom edge of quilt, lay binding around quilt to make sure that seams in binding will not end up at a corner. Adjust placement if necessary. Matching raw edges of binding to raw edge of quilt top, pin binding to right side of quilt along one edge.
2. When you reach first corner, mark $1/4$" from corner of quilt top (**Fig. 18**).

Fig. 18

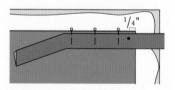

3. Beginning approximately 10" from end of binding and using $1/4$" seam allowance, sew binding to quilt, backstitching at beginning of stitching and at mark (**Fig. 19**). Lift needle out of fabric and clip thread.

Fig. 19

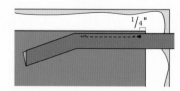

4. Fold binding as shown in **Figs. 20 – 21** and pin binding to adjacent side, matching raw edges. When you've reached the next corner, mark $1/4$" from edge of quilt top.

Fig. 20   **Fig. 21**

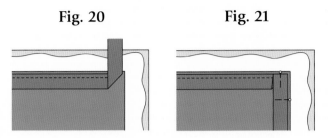

5. Backstitching at edge of quilt top, sew pinned binding to quilt (**Fig. 22**); backstitch at the next mark. Lift needle out of fabric and clip thread.

Fig. 22

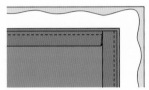

6. Continue sewing binding to quilt, stopping approximately 10" from starting point (**Fig. 23**).

Fig. 23

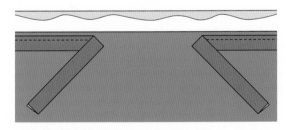

7. Bring beginning and end of binding to center of opening and fold each end back, leaving a $1/4$" space between folds (**Fig. 24**). Finger press folds.

Fig. 24

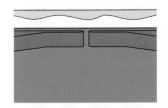

8. Unfold ends of binding and draw a line across wrong side in finger-pressed crease. Draw a line through the lengthwise pressed fold of binding at the same spot to create a cross mark. With edge of ruler at cross mark, line up 45° angle marking on ruler with one long side of binding. Draw a diagonal line from edge to edge. Repeat on remaining end, making sure that the two diagonal lines are angled the same way (**Fig. 25**).

Fig. 25

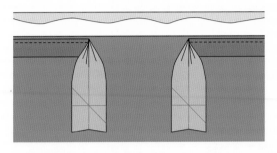

9. Matching right sides and diagonal lines, pin binding ends together at right angles (**Fig. 26**).

Fig. 26

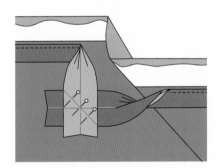

10. Machine stitch along diagonal line (**Fig. 27**), removing pins as you stitch.

Fig. 27

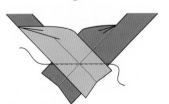

11. Lay binding against quilt to double check that it is correct length.

12. Trim binding ends, leaving $1/4$" seam allowance; press seam open. Stitch binding to quilt.

13. Trim backing and batting even with edges of quilt top.

14. On one edge of quilt, fold binding over to quilt backing and pin pressed edge in place, covering stitching line (**Fig. 28**). On adjacent side, fold binding over, forming a mitered corner (**Fig. 29**). Repeat to pin remainder of binding in place.

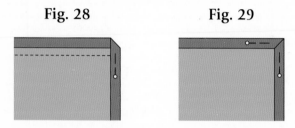

Fig. 28   **Fig. 29**

15. Blindstitch binding to backing, taking care not to stitch through to front of quilt. To Blindstitch, come up at 1, go down at 2, and come up at 3 (**Fig. 30**). Length of stitches may be varied as desired.

Fig. 30

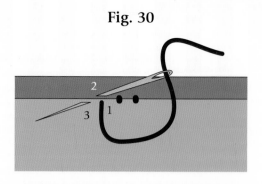

CARING FOR YOUR QUILT

- Wash finished quilt in cold water on gentle cycle with mild soap. Soaps such as Orvus® Paste or Charlie's Soap®, which have no softeners, fragrances, whiteners, or other additives, are safest. Rinse twice in cold water.

- Use a dye magnet, such as Shout® Color Catcher®, each time quilt is washed to absorb any dyes that bleed. When washing quilt the first time, you may choose to use two dye magnets for extra caution.

- Dry quilt on low heat/air fluff in 15 minute increments until dry.

Metric Conversion Chart	
Inches x 2.54 = centimeters (cm)	Yards x .9144 = meters (m)
Inches x 25.4 = millimeters (mm)	Yards x 91.44 = centimeters (cm)
Inches x .0254 = meters (m)	Centimeters x .3937 = inches (")
	Meters x 1.0936 = yards (yd)

Standard Equivalents

$1/8$"	3.2 mm	0.32 cm	$1/8$ yard	11.43 cm	0.11 m
$1/4$"	6.35 mm	0.635 cm	$1/4$ yard	22.86 cm	0.23 m
$3/8$"	9.5 mm	0.95 cm	$3/8$ yard	34.29 cm	0.34 m
$1/2$"	12.7 mm	1.27 cm	$1/2$ yard	45.72 cm	0.46 m
$5/8$"	15.9 mm	1.59 cm	$5/8$ yard	57.15 cm	0.57 m
$3/4$"	19.1 mm	1.91 cm	$3/4$ yard	68.58 cm	0.69 m
$7/8$"	22.2 mm	2.22 cm	$7/8$ yard	80 cm	0.8 m
1"	25.4 mm	2.54 cm	1 yard	91.44 cm	0.91 m